POLARITY THERAPY
HEALING WITH LIFE ENERGY

by

Alan Siegel M.Sc. N.D.

with additional material by Phil Young RPP RPE

D1292674

Published in Great Britain 2006 by

MASTERWORKS INTERNATIONAL
27 Old Gloucester Street
London
WC1N 3XX
England

Tel: 00353 (0)86 325 2645
Email: books@masterworksinternational.com
Web: http://www.masterworksinternational.com

Cover by Morag Campbell

ISBN: 0-9544450-5-8
13 digit ISBN: 978-0-9544450-5-8

This book is a revised, expanded and updated version of the book "Polarity Therapy, The Power that Heals," published by Prism Press UK, 1987.

Polarity Therapy balances and stimulates the body's life energy currents. It does not treat or diagnose illness or disease. It is not intended to be a substitute for needed medical care.

Printed in the UK/USA by Lightning Source

POLARITY THERAPY
HEALING WITH LIFE ENERGY

by Alan Siegel with additional material by Phil Young

CONTENTS

Foreword

Each of us has a healing power. We can heal ourselves, our relationships and our environment. We can help others learn to use their healing gifts and all work together to create a world of harmony and wholeness. The key lies in understanding the very nature of life itself - *energy.*

It has been said that a healthy person is one who is balanced emotionally, physically and spiritually. Most of all, if a man is healthy, he is following his own destiny, fulfiling his own potential and manifesting personal happiness and vitality in every area of his life.

As a former professor of health education at Manhattan Community College in New York, I changed careers in 1980 after studying Polarity Therapy with Pierre Pannetier N.D. and later received an N.D. degree.

Pierre Pannetier was born in Kampot, Cambodia on 1st January 1914 to a French father and a Cambodian mother. He was the fifth or eight children. His father was a surgeon, author and educator. Much of Pierre's philosophy of life came from his parents. Pierre came to the United States in 1950, after spending time in the army and in politics. In 1963 he met the founder of Polarity Therapy, Dr Randolph Stone, and shortly thereafter, began practising Polarity Therapy. In 1971 he began teaching this science.

Dr Stone spent his last two years in the United States living with Pierre and training him to be his successor before he retired to live in India in 1973. Pierre travelled extensively, giving seminars on the basics of Polarity Therapy. He also maintained a busy practice in Orange, California. He left his body on 31st October 1984 after suffering from heart failure.

Pierre taught me that Polarity Therapy is a way of life. It is a way of being in balance with life physically, mentally and spiritually. Polarity Therapy was the vehicle that I was looking for which would enable me to deliver to others the knowledge of how to be healthy. I feel privileged and blessed to have had the opportunity to study with Pierre. His love and dedication to helping others find freedom in their lives has been an inspiration to me and it is my purpose and intent to follow this path. I know that many others were helped by Pierre. He was a unique healer who taught that *love* is the true healing power. He was always a demonstration of this *love* as far as I experienced him.

As a Polarity teacher I have travelled extensively in the United States and abroad whilst I maintained a private practice in San Francisco and New York. I have been fortunate to share Polarity Therapy with over 50,000 clients and students over the years and from 1989 - 1991, I served as President of the American Polarity Therapy Association, during which time APTA adopted it's standards of Practice. After a brief retirement, I returned to teach and practice in New York before finally relocating to Mexico.

This book is dedicated to the memory of Pierre Pannetier and to the growth of Polarity Therapy around the world.

Alan Siegel
Mexico
March 2006

Alan can be contacted at alahibiscus@yahoo.com

Introduction

Dr.Randolph Stone, founder of Polarity Therapy, created this system after fifty years study and practice in the fields of medicine and the ancient healing systems of the East. Dr Stone was a chiropractor, osteopath and naturopath who practiced in Chicago, Illinois in the early part of this century. He eventually became dissatisfied with the skills he had acquired because, all too frequently, a physical adjustment would provide relief at the time but the original imbalance would recur at a later date necessitating further correction. He felt that there must be some explanation for this and so began his study of other systems of healing. His quest eventually took him to India and China in the 1930s to study the healing methods of these ancient cultures. In the late 1950s, he set down the principles of Polarity Therapy in numerous books. He finally settled in India, where he died in 1981.

Polarity Therapy is based on the theory that there is a pattern of energy in the human body which forms a matrix or blueprint that the body uses when healing itself. In the East this energy is variously called Prana, Ki or Chi but it is basically the essence of life. It is the first thing to be given and the last thing to be taken away. It is life energy.

Apart from forming a pattern, this life energy vitalises all the various physiological functions within the body. It is a moving pattern or flow of energy which gives both structure and function. The pattern of energy is prior to the physical structure, that is, the structure always reflects the energy. Should the structure become distorted through injury or disease then the energy pattern also becomes distorted. If a physical correction of some kind is then made without rebalancing the energy pattern, the energetic imbalance will continue to distort the structure, the correction will not hold and complete healing will not take place. In the normal course of events, should the flow of energy become distorted or blocked it is repaired by the master matrix which is contained deep within the unconscious mind; healing will then occur. If, for any reason, the unconscious mind cannot repair the damage, perhaps because the disruption is too great or the mental attitude has been seriously affected, then chronic health problems will arise. In Polarity Therapy we work to release these energy blocks and balance the flow so that natural healing can take place. It is because this life energy forms a link or interface between the mind and body that it is as easy to resolve emotional disturbances as it is physical imbalances by the use of Polarity techniques.

Polarity Therapy is a complete and natural system. The completeness of the system may be more easily recognised if we view a human being as comprising a physical body, energy, mind and spirit. In Polarity Therapy nutrition and exercise act on the physical body, energy is balanced, and positive thoughts and attitudes to influence the mind are developed. The combination of balancing these three aspects in turn affects the spirit. It therefore works the whole being.

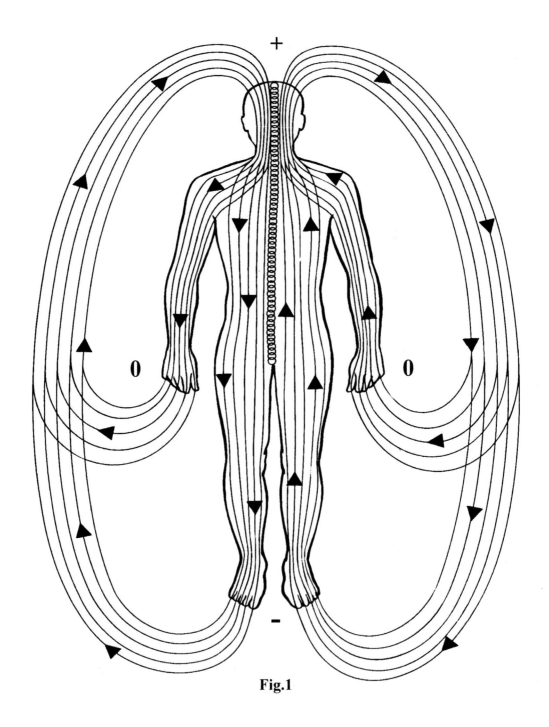

Fig.1

1 BASIC ENERGY THEORY

Before outlining the various pathways in which the life energy flows in the human body, it is important to realise that the energy interpenetrates the whole body, not only on the surface as would appear from the following illustrations. Life energy flows vertically, horizontally and spirals from the top downwards and the centre outwards. In the illustrations the polarity of the energy is given in various areas as being positive and negative; this does not mean that any particular area is literally positive or negative but is an indication of the overall direction of the flow of energy. Energy flows from positive to negative. The terms are borrowed from electromagnetic energy theory but it would be perhaps a mistake to consider life energy as electromagnetic in nature. Although not identical, there is a relationship between life energy and electromagnetic energy in as much as they follow similar laws. There is electromagnetic energy in the human body as well as life energy, each serving different purposes.

There are five, long vertical currents of energy on each side of the body. On the right side they flow down the front of the body and up the back; on the left side they flow up the front of the body and down the back (Fig. 1). Each of these currents of energy relates to an element; the elements are ether, air, fire, water and earth. Each current of energy passes through a corresponding finger and toe giving its name to the finger and toe (Fig. 2). The overall polarity of the body is shown in Fig. 1, the head being positive and the feet negative; the right side of the body is positive and the left negative. Each joint is neutral and allows a crossover of the energy currents which change polarity; this enables them to be flexible. Each finger and toe has an individual polarity as shown in Fig. 2.

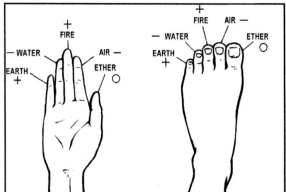

Fig.2

The names of the five elements come from the names of the 'chakras' or energy 'centres' which are located down the central or ultrasonic core energy of the body. Each chakra is a whirling vortex of energy which spins clockwise when perceived from the back. As the chakra spins it gives off a flow of energy upwards and a flow downwards, forming the long vertical currents of energy. The location of the chakras is shown in Fig. 3. Each chakra relates to the organs and functions located in its area:

Ether chakra governs the voice, hearing and throat;
Air chakra governs the circulation, heart and lungs;
Fire chakra governs the digestion, stomach and bowels;
Water chakra governs the generative organs, glandular secretions and emotional drive;
Earth chakra governs the elimination of solids and liquids, bladder and rectum.

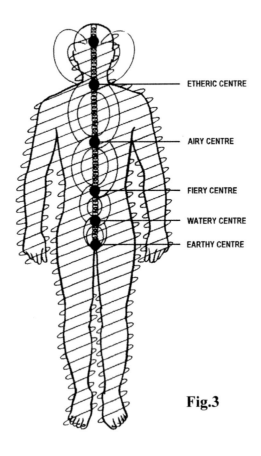

ETHERIC CENTRE

AIRY CENTRE

FIERY CENTRE

WATERY CENTRE

EARTHY CENTRE

Fig.3

The chakras are connected by a dual spiral of energy from the head downwards, the caduceus current (Fig .3). This step down of energy through the chakras shows a decreasing rate of vibration of energy, the earth chakra having the lowest level of vibration. Each of the chakras is neutral due to the crossing of the caduceus current. There are also horizontal flows of energy from right to left (Fig. 3).

It is through the umbilicus that the embryo is linked physically and energetically to the mother. All ingestion of food, oxidation and elimination takes place through the umbilicus until the baby is born and this link is cut. Even though this link is cut at birth physically this centre, and the spiral of energy that radiates outwards from the umbilicus (Fig. 4), is still of vital importance energetically to the continuing function and balance of the body. It is a primary energy pattern in the body in that it is this spiral of energy which was active when the physical structure was originally formed.

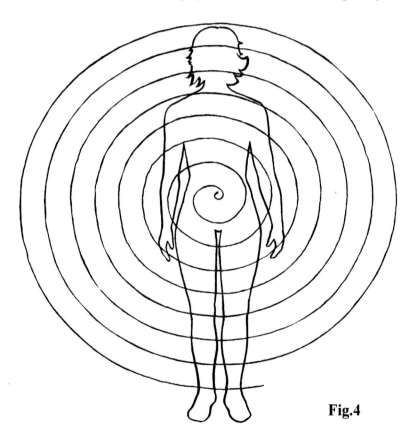

Fig.4

Each of the major cavities of the body forms what is known as an Oval Field. This is an electro-magnetic field set up by the activity of the chakras. The first field is found in the head and is known as the fire oval. The second field is the field of the throat and is called the ether oval. The third field is the chest cavity which supports the heart and lungs and is the site of the air chakra. This field is known as the air oval. The fourth oval field is situated in the upper abdomen and contains the digestive organs. It is known as the earth oval. The final field is called the water oval and is to be found in the lower abdomen in the pelvic basin. Between these oval fields are transition areas, which are usually layers of transverse muscle - the respiratory diaphragm being the most obvious. These transition areas need to be relaxed and free to enable the free flow of life energy throughout the body.

OVAL FIELDS

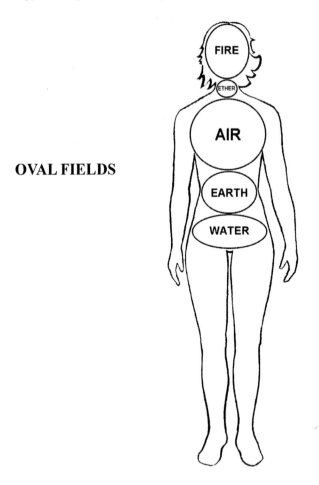

Polarity Therapy does not treat illness or disease, it treats the life energy itself which flows through and energises all the body's organs and tissues. In practice, when influencing energy, we always use bi-polar contacts, i.e., we always use two contacts on the client's body simultaneously, a positive and negative contact, be they hands or fingers or some combination of the two. A positive contact, e.g. right hand or fire finger, pushes energy and is stimulating. A negative contact, e.g. left hand or air finger, is relaxing and receives energy. When energy becomes blocked it usually registers as soreness, tenderness or pain. A simple way to bring energy to an area where it is needed is to place your left hand on the pain and right hand opposite it, either on the back, front or side of the body. This principle is used in many of the manipulations described later, such as pelvic release or the knee pain treatment.

Every part of the body has a triune relationship to other parts. This means it is either the positive, negative or neuter pole of a current of energy flowing through the body. When energy is blocked it must be released in all three places to re-establish the flow of the current. The top areas of the body are (+) and the lower areas are (-). There is also a triune relationship between the feet (-), hands (0) and body (+). Manipulations which stimulate the foot and hand poles use the principles of the reflexes located there. Reflexes are points along an energy current which connect to other points on that same current. When stimulated they can affect any other place along the same current. In addition to the feet there are reflexes in the hands as well as the arms, legs and head (see pages 146 & 147). Alternately stimulating a reflex and its corresponding body part will free blocked energy and promote normal functioning.

The science upon which the manipulations are based involves the use of triune relationships, reflexes and/or opposite positive and negative contacts. The negative poles are the most frequently obstructed. They should be stimulated first, then the positive pole in order to send currents over the entire circuit. When diagonal contacts are used on the body, it is the serpentine brain wave (caduceus) currents that are activated (Fig. 3). The purpose of polarity manipulation is to locate blocked energy and, using the principles outlined above, release it. When energy is released, the organs and systems tend to normalise their functions and healing can take place naturally.

2 THE LAW OF POLARITY

Polarity Therapy works with the finer essences of matter. In science, physics especially, the same principles upon which Polarity are based have been utilised in atomic and nuclear research. Yet according to Dr Stone their application in healing is far from being fully realised. Paramahansa Yogananda said that the medicine of the future would be electricity and rays first and, as we become more advanced, thoughts will be used to heal. Here he is speaking of the same finer vibratory essences which constitute matter.

At this time a dedicated Polarity practitioner might be frustrated in his/her attempt to delve deeply into the consideration of these subtle energies and how Polarity Therapy affects them, as there is not a great deal written on the matter. The following material is based on a 1976 discussion by Pierre Pannetier and should shed some light as to why Polarity Therapy is the powerful healing science that it is. Pierre Pannetier said:

The two brushing manipulations at the end of the General Treatment gave me the key. They are an example of correct polarity. Using this law of Polarity helps produce quicker results in terms of energy flow. Remember that your relaxation is prior to the law of Polarity.

To begin, we will take the example of an active magnet. In the magnet energy flows from one pole to the other through the neuter pole. If we cut the magnet in half, we change the poles and create another full magnet. No matter how many times we do this the result is the same: a magnet is created with a positive, negative, and neuter pole (see magnets in diagram opposite).

In the human body there are trillions of cells and countless atoms within each cell. Every cell and every atom is positive (+), negative (-) and neuter (0), just like an active magnet. In Dr Stone's book, 1971 Private Notes for Students of Polarity Therapy, he reprints some of the writings from Dr Babbitt's classic book, Principles of Light and Color, written in 1886. Here Dr Babbitt describes how the atoms, each being (+), (-) and (0), stick together laterally and longitudinally, by attraction or magnetism, and he explains how electromagnetic currents flow through the body. (Dr Babbitt used colour and light to heal the body - the same healing energy we use in Polarity Therapy.)

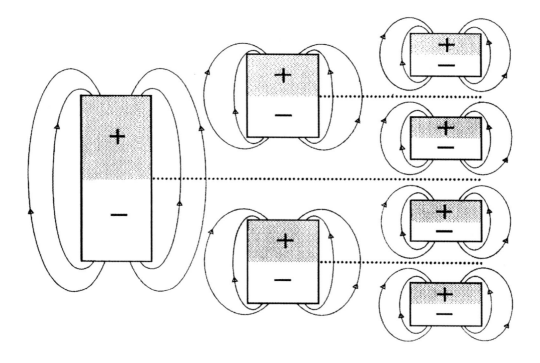

By the placement of our hands on the prescribed areas of the body, we redirect the flow of energy to where it is needed, creating new currents in the body. According to Dr Stone these currents, which are created by the union of two different polarities, flow from one primary current in the middle of the body. The new currents can flow in all directions, not just with the wireless currents referred to by Dr Stone (vertical, spiral, horizontal and caduceus currents). They can flow from front to back, up or down, side to side, etc., depending upon where we place our hands. It is important to mention here that if we fail to use the correct polarity of our contacts the energy will still flow, though the reaction will be slower. This is so because, although the body as a single unit is divided into polarities, if we look at it on a cellular or atomic level we see that, if we place our hands anywhere on the body, we are, in fact, in contact with thousands of positive, negative, and neuter poles at the same time. The process by which these currents are created is called induction. This is an important concept to understand.

For myself, clarifying the meaning of induction meant looking in the dictionary for each word within the definition that was unclear to me. Within the definition of these words were other words to look up. After several hours the process of induction which occurs in Polarity Therapy became clear to me, as well as much of Dr Stone's material of which I was previously uncertain.

Webster's Dictionary defines induction as 'the generation of electromagnetic force in a closed circuit by a varying magnetic flux through the circuit'. Electromagnetic force (EMF) is the energy that is created from chemical and mechanical energy by a battery, the life energy we are balancing in Polarity Therapy. Our hands are batteries which create a flux or flow of energy through the closed circuit or wireless currents of energy. The healing energy is transmitted from one contact to the other by flowing through the atoms and cells which are connected by magnetism or the attraction of their opposite poles.

Our bodies are like the core of an electromagnet. Both have a positive and negative pole. The electromagnet has a coil of insulated wire around it, which corresponds to the life energy currents which magnetise our body. This makes our body capable of attracting to itself whatever it needs, just as an electromagnet attracts iron and other materials to itself. What makes this possible is the motion and alignment of the atomic electrons and their surrounding field. When our life energy is not flowing well, the physical body's ability to attract what it needs is impaired. The result is pain, stress and dis-ease. In Polarity Therapy we stimulate, unblock and balance the energy, bringing to the cells, tissues and organs of the body what they need in order to function normally.

The key to health, therefore, is to keep the life energy, or prana, flowing in the body. This was the basis for all the ancient healing arts. Free-flowing energy enables every particle and cell in our body to attract what it needs in order to function according to its design. In Polarity Therapy we follow this principle through manipulations with our hands, exercise, proper diet and right living, combined with the positive power of mind. Here, now, are some basic guidelines for applying the law of Polarity to Polarity manipulations.

When placing your hands on the body you are, in effect, cutting a magnet in half, meaning that the poles change according to where you place your hands. The best contacts on the body are positive to negative. This creates a balanced (neuter) pole which can then be combined with a contact to any area of the body. This is the law of Polarity. When you have one contact on a neuter place on the body, you can combine it with a positive or negative hand or finger on any other part of the body. Your thumbs, being neuter, can be anything you need, (+ or -). You can combine a thumb contact with any other finger (+ or -).

The most balanced and stable places in the body are the neuter points. They are created by a crossover of energy currents in the body, changing from positive to negative and vice versa. The neuter places include all the joints, the navel, the chakras and a vertical line in the middle of the body which is one and a half to two inches wide. Currents of energy will flow from any blocked area by contacting that area with the nearest joint or the navel. With one hand or finger stimulate the energy block and with the other hand or finger, alternately stimulate the neuter point. Remember to be very gentle with the contacts.

In Polarity Therapy the higher contact on the body, or the one closest to the head is always the positive pole. The lower contact is the negative pole. For example, if you are standing on the client's right side (she is on her back) with your left hand on her shoulder and your right hand on her hip, your left hand is on the positive pole (her shoulder) and your right hand is on the negative pole (her hip). If your left hand moves to her hip and your right hand moves to her knee, the hip is now the positive pole and the knee is the negative. In using the law of Polarity always consider the higher contact. Thus, standing on the client's right side which is positive, a contact with your left hand (higher contact) which is negative, creates a balanced effect. This is what we want whenever possible. The lower hand, in this case the right hand, can then go anywhere on the body below the left hand. So we have these two important rules to remember when a client is lying on her back:

don't cross the mid-line of the body;
don't cross your hands on the body.

When the client is on her abdomen, the rule changes slightly. In order to have the correct polarity with the upper hand, you must cross the middle of the body with your hands. For example, if you are standing on the client's left side you would contact her right shoulder with your left hand by reaching across the spine. Your right hand could then be placed anywhere below the left hand.

Following these guidelines will help the energy to flow. But don't get too bogged down by specifics. Remember - you will always be contacting positive, negative and neuter poles, no matter where you place your hands on the body. And always keep in mind that *your own relaxation is the most important factor* in utilising the Law of Polarity.

If you are tense whilst giving a treatment then the Law of Polarity will not come into effect and the induction of new energy currents will be impaired.

3 THE FIVE ELEMENTS

In their approach to diagnosis and treatment some Polarity therapists will use a primarily intuitive approach, others will use reflex theory but perhaps by far the largest group will use five element theory for diagnosis and determining which treatments are appropriate. Any approach to treatment is valid. The ultimate goal is the client's return to health. The path taken to reach this goal is of little importance. Ultimately, intuition will play a great part in whatever approach is used - five elements or otherwise.

Dr Stone himself used the five-element approach. He took it from the Ayurvedic system of medicine which he was exposed to during his time in India. In the Ayurvedic system all matter and energy is classified as consisting of the five elements. As given earlier these are ether, air, fire, water and earth. Each element has a particular 'chakra' or energy centre that relates to it. Each element has various physiological functions associated with it as follows:

ETHER ELEMENT All the various networks that pervade the entire body, e.g. nerves, veins, arteries, etc. It is also represented in all the joints; it is the space (ether) between the various bones that give flexibility.

AIR ELEMENT The breath and circulation through the nervous system and blood vessels, and the movement provided by the mind operating through the nervous system and the parasympathetic branch of the autonomic nervous system.

FIRE ELEMENT The heat within the body generated by the digestive fluids as they perform the digestive function. The sympathetic branch of the autonomic nervous system and the basic energy level of the body, the vitality.

WATER ELEMENT All the soft body material, the skin, muscle tissue, etc. All the fluids: lymph, blood and mucous secretions. It also gives the basic matrix which binds the physical structure together.

EARTH ELEMENT All the solid bony material which gives the body its basic structure and support for all the body organs. It also governs elimination processes.

The ether element, because of its all pervasive presence, can be considered as the mother of the other four elements. Each of the remaining four elements has an astrological triad associated with it and a particular body part which relates to the astrological sign (sun sign). These correspondences are as follows:

Air element: Gemini (shoulders), Libra (kidneys), Aquarius (ankles);
Fire element: Aries (eyes), Leo (solar plexus), Sagittarius (thighs);
Water element: Cancer (breasts); Scorpio (genitals), Pisces (feet);
Earth element: Taurus (neck), Virgo (bowels), Capricorn (knees).

From a person's sun sign one can see which element was predominant in the outer world at the time of their birth, and the body parts which relate to it. Very often a person from under any particular element will have a tendency or sensitivity to developing problems in one of the three body parts as listed above. The disturbance may register in either the positive, neutral or negative pole, e.g. a person from under the sun sign Capricorn might develop problems in the neck (positive pole), bowels (negative pole) or the knees (neutral pole) or any combination of three.

In the Ayurvedic system the five elements are often grouped together to form what are called the three *principles* or *doshas*; these are called Air, Fire and Water. The Air principle is formed by the combination of the ether and air elements. The Fire principle is formed only by the fire element. The Water principle is formed by the combination of the water and earth elements.

The Air principle governs the total nervous activity in the body and also the gaseous matter in the body. The body parts related to the Air principle are the chest, bowels and calves. The Fire principle governs all the catabolic processes in the body, i.e. the breakdown of food into usable materials and the heat within the body. The body parts related to the Fire principle are the head (including the eyes) and the digestive system, stomach, pancreas, liver, etc. The Fire principle also relates to the conscious will and intellect. The Water principle governs the physical structure of the body, all the alkaline bodily secretions and the anabolic processes in the body, i.e. the growth of new tissue and ongoing repair work. The major body area related to the Water principle is the pelvis.

All disease can be viewed as being either an excess or depletion of activity in one or more of the three principles, or a disturbance in the functioning of one or more of the five elements. The art of five-element diagnosis lies in the understanding of the ways in which the elements interact with each other. As the energy moves through the elements, starting with ether, it is first given out by the ether chakra which energises the related body functions. The energy then flows back to the centre to be sent down to energise the next lower chakra, in this case the air chakra, and so on. The energy is stepped down through each chakra and element.

With this in mind it is easy to see how a blockage in the outward or inward flow of energy in any particular element can result in an excess of energy in the elements above the blockage and a depletion of energy in the elements below the blockage. As well as the energy feeding downwards through the elements, the function of each element controls or balances the element above it. If we take as an analogy a car engine, we can relate the ether element to the electrical system, the air element to the air intake through the carburettor, the fire element to the combustion at the piston heads, the water element to the cooling system and the earth element to the exhaust system.

Using this analogy we can see how each element feeds the next and also how they control each other: water (coolant) controls fire (engine temperature), for example. Many other interactions can be seen as well, an excess of water will cool fire giving incomplete combustion and poor elimination (earth-exhaust). A depletion of air (too lean a mixture) will give weak fire (incomplete combustion) and so on. One can also look at nature itself to see other interactions, for example, air refreshes earth as any gardener knows how important it is to aerate the soil. When you see laundry drying outside on a windy day you are looking at an excess of air drying out water. The examples around you are endless, simply because everything can be viewed as being composed of the five elements.

In the life-energy balancing techniques in this book you will find treatments that affect the three principles and the five elements. After the General Energy Balancing Session and the balancing treatments that follow, the treatment of the air principle is covered from p. 64 to 70; the fire principle treatments from p.70 to 77; the water principle from p. 78 to 82. Then come the elemental treatment; ether from p. 83 to 91; air from p. 92 to 110; fire from p. 112; water from p. 113 to 123 and earth from p.124 to 131.

The treatments which follow after this are structural, and can considered to be of the earth element. The last two treatments are based on reflex theory. This classification is very broad because often in a treatment there is. a balancing of two elements, e.g. coccyx treatment which is a balancing of water and earth (or water and fire) though it is listed as an earth treatment

The colon treatment is actually a treatment which effects the air principle as it relates to the bowels (earth) so it too is listed under earth, though it is an air principle treatment. The knee-pain treatment is listed under earth, because the knee is part of the earth triad, but it could be considered an ether treatment.

There is a great deal more that could be said concerning the five elements but it would be beyond the scope of this book to go into the subject in any greater detail. Any good book on Ayurvedic medicine will offer many fascinating insights for the Polarity therapist.

4 THE THREE MODES OF TOUCH

It goes without saying that the way that you touch someone whether it be in the therapeutic context or in the more intimate context of a personal relationship is extremely important. Through the medium of touch we can convey a whole gamut of messages, a silent communication takes place every time we place our hands on another human being and as with verbal communication, touch can elicit a whole range of responses in answer to that contact.

When we place our hands on another human being in Polarity we have a special responsibility to be 'present' in our hands as we work. We need to be sensitive to the feedback from the tissues beneath our fingers in order that we may physically dialogue with them effectively, such as when we coax tense and held muscles to relax and soften, but we also have to be mindful of the emotional communication that is also a big part of the work. It is therefore pertinent to take a good look at the three modes of touch utilised in Polarity and to consider their use and their communication pattern to the client.

The three Gunas are Sanskrit words for the three energies of the Universe and are therefore representative of our three polarities. Satva is the neuter pole of the mind principle sustained by a ray from the Creator. Rajas is the positive pole which is the restless drive of the emotions and the desire for action and fulfilment. Tamas is the precipitate of these two, inertia, darkness, resistance and the reaction to all action. We apply these three categories to the method of touch that we employ in Polarity.

SATVIC touch is categorised as neutral and is generally described as balancing. Returning to this mode of touch after stimulating or releasing the body allows the energy to disperse and move where it needs to go. It is also an opportunity for the practitioner to "listen" to the feed back from the body and then act accordingly. The touch can range from a deep contactful hold or moulding to the body through to extremely light contact just at the surface of the skin and even off the body altogether. There is no movement involved. The practitioners hands just rest with the client and allow the energy to express itself in whatever way is appropriate. Even though this touch is described as balancing there is nothing weak about it. This neutral touch is full of potential energy. Within this neutrality there is a resonance with the core energy and the Source and because all undifferentiated energy is present in this neutrality all things are possible. The ether energy held here encourages an openness and expansion of the energy fields to allow for the interplay of the other elemental energies. With this openness comes the potential for the air energy to create movement and change. The fire energy can then be released to warm the body. This warmth activates the water energy and promotes an easier flow of fluids through the body. The earth energy is represented by the release of old toxins through the organs of elimination. Satvic touch gives the body time and space to reorganise itself to a higher level of adaptability. This mode of touch which is more about 'being' than 'doing' also needs to convey a sense of safety and support in the face of all this opening.

RAJASIC touch is described as positive and is designed to stimulate and mobilise the energy allowing it to expand outward (centrifugally) from the centre. The touch involves a range of movements from small circular, *almost* massage like technique, done with individual fingers over a small area, through to larger movements involving rocking the entire body. Movement is the key word here. By moving we are introducing the air element to our client to elicit a response from their energy. When stimulating a small area with the fingers it is important to move the underlying tissue and not just the skin. When larger whole body rocking is called for then it is important to rock the body at its natural frequency. In purely physical terms it requires the least effort on the part of the practitioner when you rock the clients body in this way. This allows you to maintain a high level of sensitivity to any subtle shifts or changes in the holding patterns within the clients' body. When rocked at this frequency, which is dependant on the size, weight and tension pattern of the client, a loosening of the emotional and physical holding is much more likely to occur as the client relaxes into the comfort and ease of this natural rhythm. If we impose our own frequency of movement on to the client then the movement can feel uncomfortable and sometimes be disturbing to them creating more tension and holding.

TAMASIC touch is described as deep and dispersing. This mode of touch is used primarily to break up long standing holding and tension in the physical body. It facilitates the return of long stored energy back to the core (centripetal flow). This is a more invasive technique than the previous two and the practitioner should be aware of this. Hard, dehydrated tissue does not readily surrender to persistent, hard pressure, which can be extremely painful causing the client to pull away.

When performing tamasic bodywork you should only apply pressure for short periods of time (30 seconds to 1 minute) then release the hold and allow the body to adjust and relax before reapplying another short application to the tissues.

One other point, communication is in the feedback and touch is no different to verbal dialogue in this regard. Listen to the message that your clients' body is giving you and respond with your touch. If the conversation doesn't flow then change the message you are giving and convey that through your hands.

5 LIFE ENERGY BALANCING TECHNIQUES

The explanation and illustrations for all the manipulations have been carefully done. It is my wish that anyone reading this will be able to follow the step-by-step instructions and give a very effective Polarity session.

For each manipulation the following procedure, when applicable, will be used:

Name of the manipulation.
Discussion of the theory and purpose of the manipulation.
The position the client is in during the manipulation.
Step-by-step instructions for each manipulation.
How these principles can be used for other treatments.
Nutritional guidance to enhance the Polarity session.

Keep in mind that Polarity Therapy treats energy flowing through organs and not organs themselves. For example, a colon treatment treats energy flowing through the colon not the colon itself.

The term 'client' will be used to refer to the person receiving the session. The manipulations are described as if a table for the bodywork session is being used. Polarity sessions can effectively be given on the floor or on a bed. All that is needed is a logical adjustment by the person giving the session, e.g. kneeling at client's side as opposed to standing. Before you begin, look over the points to remember when giving a Polarity treatment.

Most of the manipulations involve stimulation of points or areas. Unless you are instructed to stimulate an area in a certain way or in a certain direction, do what feels comfortable and natural. You can stimulate forward and backwards, in circular movements, or by gentle pressing and releasing.

The most important aspect of stimulation is gentleness. Let your fingers and hands be soft. Allow them to mould to the client's body. Remember that you can be firm and go deep with your touch and still be gentle. Make sure never to use force as this creates tension and blocks life energy.

Polarity Therapy works with the life energy or vibration. This is the power that heals. Love and gentleness are always more effective in creating positive change than using force.

It has been my experience that the flow of life energy to any part of the body can be enhanced by 'feeling.' To do this requires concentration. What I do is as follows: after stimulating alternate points I hold the two contacts (without stimulating). I then concentrate on the point between my eyebrows and visualise energy or light flowing from my brain to my hands and through them to my client's body. Practice this 'feeling' technique and see what results you get. I offer it as a very useful adjunct to Polarity Therapy. It has had miraculous results for me.

THE GENERAL ENERGY BALANCING SESSION

This general session is presented almost exactly the way it was taught to me by Pierre Pannetier, my wonderful Polarity Therapy teacher. The general session primarily stimulates the long vertical currents of energy by contacts at various negative, positive and neuter poles. I use the general Session as a framework for most of my Polarity sessions. I then include some specific manipulations. The general session is a complete treatment of life energy by itself and will produce a highly relaxed and happy client when done correctly and with love.

Because we work with vibration, we affect the mind as well as the body since thoughts and matter are all composed of the same universal energy. The only difference is in the rate of vibration.

The general session can take from 15 to 45 minutes depending on how quickly the manipulations are done. As a general rule, I recommend working on a client's body for about an hour. Young children and senior citizens should be worked on for less time. A half-hour session is usually sufficient. These are suggested guidelines only. Use common sense and intuition to help you.

Points to Remember When Giving a Polarity Therapy Session

1. Have a clean, quiet, simply furnished room to work in.
2. Prepare yourself by meditating or sitting quietly for five minutes prior to the treatment.
3. Greet your client with a smile, warmth and love.
4. Ask them to undress to their underclothing and lie on their back on the table. (clients can wear loose clothing if they prefer).
5. Cover their body with a sheet or blanket.
6. Ask them to let you know if any place that you touch is sensitive or painful.
7. When doing the manipulations, relax your hands and mould them to your client's body.

8. Be careful not to cross your hands on your client's body.

9. When stimulating points, use the fleshy pads of your fingers.

10. Use a very gentle touch, never force. Force creates tension which blocks energy.

11. A light and gentle touch moves energy by introducing the air element (which provides movement). Be aware that the healing does not come from you. It is the life energy that heals

12. When stimulating any body part remember that you are not giving a massage. In massage your hands slide over the body. In polarity our hands or fingers stay on the same area of skin and move the skin over the underlying structures. Always keep in mind that we are influencing energy.

13. Understand that we all heal at different rates, therefore don't expect to see a physical result after you do a manipulation. This means that you should be neutral when working on your client.

14. Concentrate on feeling energy which is experienced as a tingling or a warmth between your hands and your client's body.

15. With most manipulations, stimulate for a couple of minutes, then just hold and feel the energy. Hold for 30 seconds to 1 minute and move to another manipulation. If after stimulating for 2 minutes you feel no energy, hold for 1 minute longer and then move on.

16. Once you feel energy moving you've achieved the result of the manipulation. The life energy has intelligence. Once aroused it will know what to do and where to go.

17. If the manipulations don't seem to work, place your hands on your client's body and send love. visualise energy flowing through your hands to your client.

18. Clients may or may not talk; they may even fall asleep. There is no particular way they should act. The important key is their comfort and relaxation.

19. You can't change the direction in which life energy flows in the body with these manipulations. You can only effect the intensity of it

OUTLINE OF THE GENERAL ENERGY BALANCING SESSION

SEATED AT CLIENT'S HEAD
1 Cradle occipital bone in palms of hands. Tips of air fingers on juncture of neck and shoulders. Thumbs alongside air fingers.
2 Right hand grasps occiput with thumb and air finger. Left hand on forehead, thumb on front fontanel.

STANDING ON CLIENT'S RIGHT SIDE
3 Left hand on forehead, right hand rocks abdomen below navel.

SEATED OR STANDING AT CLIENT'S FEET
4 Alternately stimulate inside ankle points with foot flexion.
5 Alternately stimulate outside ankle points with foot extension.
6 Stimulate top of ankle with both thumbs.
7 Alternate toe stretches with compression on top and bottom toe tendons using thumb and air fingers.
8 Toe pulls - with toe taut give quick short pull
9 Leg pull with foot flexed on exhale.
10-15 Repeat this sequence on the opposite foot.

STANDING ON RIGHT SIDE OF CLIENT
16 Left hand on pelvis. Right hand rocks leg.
17 Wrist flip.
18 Arm and shoulder rotations while holding wrist.
19 Finger and arm stretch.
20 Thumb and web contact.
21 Alternate thumb and web contact with inside-elbow reflex point.
22 Hold elbow. Place thumb over tendons below elbow Alternate stimulation on elbow, while rocking abdomen below lower ribs.
23 Contact on shoulder and opposite pelvic bone. Rock and stretch.
24-30 Repeat this sequence of manipulations on client's left side.

This is the time for specific manipulations.

CLOSING MANIPULATIONS DONE SEATED AT CLIENT'S HEAD

31 Right fire finger stimulates right occipital point. Left air finger between nose and right eyebrow.

32 Repeat on left side. Switch hands.

33 Thumbs in front Fontanel, little fingers on the jaw joint.

34 Right hand grasps occipital ridge with thumb and air finger. Left thumb in front Fontanel; other fingers like a claw on forehead.

STANDING ON CLIENT'S RIGHT SIDE

35 Chakra balance. Left thumb between eyebrows, right thumb in navel.

CLIENT SEATED

36 Back brushing.

37 Front brushing.

38 Big hug.

MANIPULATION 1: OCCIPUT AND TENTH CRANIAL NERVE

This first manipulation introduces the client to your touch and allows you to tune into them. It begins the process of opening up the energy flows. By satvically holding the head and tuning into its energy an energetic impulse is sent down to the feet on the basis of a geometric reflex pattern*. This hold stimulates the occipital area of the skull which is a para-sympathetic nervous system reflex area, which begins a relaxation response in the client. The tips of the air fingers, which touch the juncture of the head and neck, also activate the vagus nerve (10th cranial nerve), which is the major nerve of this branch of the nervous system. If the energetic response is weak a gentle rhythmic compression can be applied to the side of the neck with the air fingers. It is important when doing this manipulation to establish a baseline of energetic activity in the client which will give you something to measure against by the end of the session when you come back to the cranium. This will help to establish how effective your session has been with regard to stimulating and balancing the energy flow.

Ref: Anterior/posterior Geometric Reflexes, appendix Chart E

Client is on her back throughout the General Session.

Step 1 Sit at client's head.
    2 Lift her head with your right hand and gently place your overlapped hands (Fig. 5) under the head.

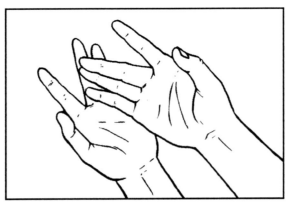

Fig.5

Step 3 Your index or air fingers touch the place where her neck and shoulder meet. This is a point along the pathway of the tenth cranial (vagus) nerve as it runs from the head to the torso (Fig. 6).

4 Client's occipital bone is cradled in your overlapped hands.

5 Your thumbs are next to your air or index fingers, but are not touching her head (Fig, 6).

6 Hold this position for several minutes. See if you can feel a tingling or warm sensation where your fingers touch her shoulders.

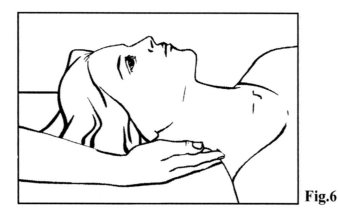

Fig.6

MANIPULATION 2: FOREHEAD AND OCCIPUT

This manipulation enhances the polarisation of the front of the body (sensory) in relation to the energy currents on the back of the body (motor). The left hand, being negatively charged, enhances the negative charge on the front of the head and the positively charged right hand enhances the positive charge on the back of the head. Simultaneously, it also balances the top of the head (motor) in relation to the energy currents lower on the head (sensory) as the left hand, being negatively charged, balances the positively charged forehead and the positively charged right hand balances the negatively charged occiput. The long line currents which pass over the top of the skull on both sides are activated by this hold. As the hands are diagonally opposite each other there is also an activation of the deep spiral currents of energy known as the Caduceus currents that begin in the cranium and flow in a spiral down through the body. The thumb contact engages the ultra-sonic core energy.

When hooking the occipital area with the thumb and air finger, apply a slight traction to the occipital base to create a slight separation or widening of the relationship between the atlas and the occipital base, thereby opening the foramen magnum. This will help the energy to flow through the neck and into the head.

The placement of the thumb on the fontanel is dependent on the size your hands and the clients head. It is not necessary that it actually touches that area just that it points to that particular place. It is more important that your hand contacts the forehead.

Step 1 Sit at client's head,
    2 Place your right hand under her neck.
    3 Slide your right hand up towards her head until your thumb and air fingers hook the occipital ridge. The occipital ridge is the lowest edge of the cranial bone (occipital bone) which is at the base of the skull Client's head should rest gently in the palm of your right hand (Fig. 7).
    4 Place your left palm on her forehead. Your left thumb will contact the front fontanel. This is the soft spot on a baby's head and can be felt in older people as an indentation between the cranial bones. It is in the centre of the head about 1.5 inches from the hair line. This contact stimulates the cranial fluid which surrounds the brain.
    5 Hold until you feel energy as a tingling sensation, or for 2 minutes.

Fig.7

MANIPULATION 3: TUMMY ROCK

The manipulation known as the Tummy rock involves placing the left hand on the forehead and the right hand between the pelvic crests. This manipulation, which involves rocking the abdomen and pelvis, is a balancing of the fire oval of the head with the water oval of the pelvis. It also generally helps to free the pelvis such that the energy will easily flow down through both legs as well as up through the body. This is a top bottom balance, the left hand (negative) on the top of the body and the right hand (positive) on the lower part of the body beneath the diaphragm (negative). This is the first time that rajasic stimulating touch is used in the general session.

Step 1 Stand on client's right side.
2 Place the palm of your left hand on her forehead.
3 Place your right hand palm down, just below the navel (Fig.8).
4 Rock the abdomen without actually sliding your right hand. Do this for two minutes. The whole body should gently rock.
5 Stop, hold without stimulation and feel the energy. Try closing your eyes when feeling for the movement of energy.

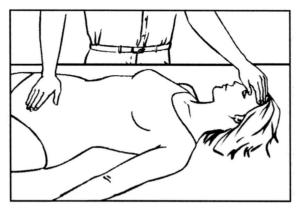

Fig.8

MANIPULATION 4: INSIDE ANKLE WITH FLEXION OF THE FOOT

This manipulation stimulates the energy flowing through the ankle. After some general massage work on the feet to encourage relaxation and increase awareness of this often neglected area begin to rajasically stimulate the inside of the ankle combined with flexion of the foot. This technique mainly focuses on stimulating the various reflexes around the inside of the ankle*. The reflexes in question are to the rectum, womb and prostate. As you hold the ball of the foot and flex the ankle you are also stimulating the air element as the ankle is the negative pole of the astrological triad of air, and the ball of the foot reflexes to the chest. The technique also influences the head through geometric relationship.* When a client is relaxed you will notice that the foot flexion will always make the head nod. If the head does not move look for tension further up the body.

Ref: Foot Reflexes, appendix Chart F & anterior/posterior Geometric Reflexes, appendix Chart E

Step 1 Stand at client's feet.
    2 Hold the heel of her right foot in your right hand (Fig.9).
    3 Place the heel of your left hand on the ball of client's right foot.
    4 With your left hand flex her foot towards her head.
    5 Release the flexed position of the foot and at the same time press on the areas indicated by an (x) with your right thumb.

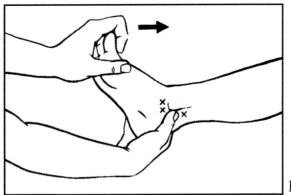

Fig.9

Step 6 Repeat the flexion of the foot and alternately press on the contact areas indicated as you release the flexion. Continue back and forth around the ankle areas indicated by (x's). Repeat 3 to 4 times.

MANIPULATION 5: OUTSIDE ANKLE WITH FOOT EXTENSION

This manipulation works around the bone on the outside of the ankle. This technique is similar to the previous one except that in this case the foot is extended towards you. The reflexes stimulated here are the kidneys, the ovaries, testes, the hip joint and the valves of the colon*. The extension or flexion of the feet helps to lift the reflexes to the surface.

Ref: Foot Reflexes, appendix Chart F

Step 1 Stand at client's feet.
    2 Hold heel of client's right foot in your left hand (Fig. 10).
    3 Place your right hand on the instep of her right foot.
    4 Extend the foot by gently pulling it down and towards you.
    5 As you release the extension press on the ankle areas indicated by (x's) with your thumb.

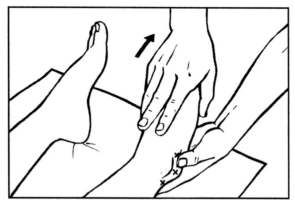

Fig.10

Step 6 Alternately extend the foot and press around the ankle areas indicated with your left thumb as you release the extension. This is the same procedure as in Manipulation 4 except that you are extending the foot instead of flexing it.

7 Go around the ankle 3-4 times.

MANIPULATION 6: ANKLE ROTATION

This manipulation involves contacting the point at the indentation on the top of the ankle which has a definite reflex action to the valves of the colon, the diaphragm and top line of the shoulders*. The top line of the shoulders is also an activation or reflex area for the Para- sympathetic nervous system.

*Ref: Evolutionary Reflexes, appendix Chart C

Step 1 Stand at client's feet.

2 Place both your thumbs in the hollow space on top of the right ankle (Fig.11).

3 Your other fingers rest gently on either side of the ankle.

4 Stimulate the top of the ankle in a clockwise direction 10 times. Reverse direction and stimulate the top of the ankle counter-clockwise 10 times Stimulate with enough pressure so that you rock client's body gently from side to side.

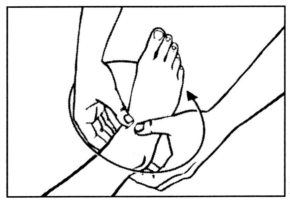

Fig.11

MANIPULATION 7: TOE STRETCHES AND TENDON COMPRESSION

Toe stretch and tendon compression affects the five bi-lateral long line currents of energy, as they run through the toes, thus influencing all the five elements. It also stimulates all the reflexes in the feet and so influences the whole body. The energy can get easily stuck in the small joints of the toes and it is important to release them for greater energy flow.

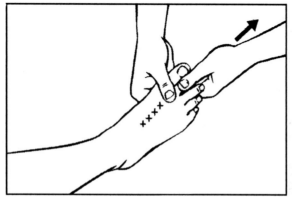

Fig.12

Step 1 Stand at client's feet.

    2 With your left hand grasp the big toe of client's right foot. Hold it as close to the foot as possible (Fig. 12). Rotate the toe 3 – 4 times in each direction.

    3 Your right hand is on the foot with your thumb on top and your air or index finger underneath it. Both fingers are on the tendons which connect to the toe.

    4 With your left hand stretch the toe by pulling it towards you.

    5 Release the stretch and simultaneously compress the tendons by pressing your thumb and air fingers towards each other. Start close to the toe.

    6 Repeat this alternate stretching of the toe and compression of the tendon as you move down the foot inch by inch towards the ankle. Do this 3-4 times.

    7 Repeat steps 1-4 on each toe. Remember to alternate. Stretch the toe and, when you relax it, compress the tendons. You may change hands to accommodate large feet, e.g. right hand on toe and left hand on the tendons.

MANIPULATION 8: TOE PULLS

Once the toes have been loosened we can perform the toe pulls. This tamasic technique has a powerful tonic effect on the body. In a healthy person the toe joints are usually loose and will click easily on extension. It is possible that any one or all of the three toe joints may click. The tension in the toes and which joints click can be a useful diagnostic factor as each toe relates to an element and body part. It is important that the toes are kept free as they are important cross over points where the long line currents change direction and the energy changes character from motor(centrifugal) to sensory (centripetal) energy. They also suffer greatly from being squashed into shoes for the best part of the day.

Step 1 Stand at client's feet.
    2 Grasp the big toe of client's foot with both of your hands. Hold the toe as close to the foot as possible with your thumbs overlapped on top of the toe (Fig.13)
    3 Stretch the toe towards you until it is taut with no slack.
    4 With the toe taut, pull it quickly towards you a distance of 1/2 inch. Be sure not to slide your hands on the toe. Use the sheet under your fingers if toes feel slippery so you have a better grip.
    5 Sometimes the toes make a popping sound as you pull them. This is caused by gas flowing into the space created by the pull of the toe. It is quite common and is no cause for concern. As a general rule do not pull arthritic or damaged toes just give them a good stretch.

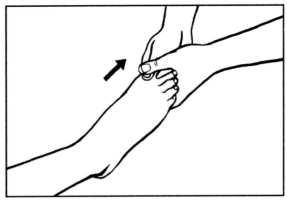

Fig.13

MANIPULATION 9: LEG PULL

The leg pull is a specific adjustment for a high arch in the foot but it is a beneficial technique for the whole leg as it causes a gentle separation of the joints of the ankle, knee and hip. The hand position on top of the foot reflexes to the middle back. The technique can be done slightly lower on the foot (closer to the ankle) with the middle finger influencing the cuboid bone, in which case it is a powerful stimulation of the kidney area. It can also be used to re-position the talus and the tibia bone if there is difficulty in ankle flexion due to bone misalignment. When pulling the leg, only use enough force to effectively separate and free the joints, relying on the body's self regulating ability to affect re-alignment where necessary.

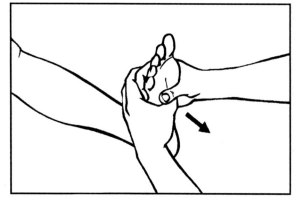

Fig.14

Step 1 Stand at client's feet.
    2 Grasp the right foot with both your hands. Your palms are overlapped on the instep of the foot. Your thumbs are below the ball of the foot (Fig. 14).
    3 Ask client to inhale. As she does flex her foot as you bend it towards her head.
    4 Ask her to exhale. Just before she has exhaled all the air in her lungs, and with the foot still flexed, pull the entire leg towards you 1 inch. It is a quick short pull. Hold this position for several seconds and then release your grip.

MANIPULATIONS 10-15

After completing Manipulation 9, repeat Manipulations 4-9 on client's left foot. The procedure is exactly the same except that you substitute the right hand for the left and vice versa.

MANIPULATION 16: PELVIS AND KNEE ROCK

As well as freeing the hip joint and stimulating the energy of the legs, this is a balancing of the earth element as the Astrological triad for the earth element is knees, bowels and neck. The freeing of the hip joint will in turn affect the tempo-mandibular joint at the jaw. Tension in the hip is often reflected by tension in the jaw and vice versa. As a variation, the hand on the leg can be repositioned at several places along the leg whilst rocking, in which case there is more of an influence on the fire energy in the thighs.

Step 1 Stand at client's right side.
    2 Place your left hand on the inside of her right pelvic bone, palm down and fingers pointed towards her feet. This is called Poupart's ligament (Fig. 15).
    3 Your right hand is just above the knee on the outside of her right leg.
    4 Gently rock the leg with your right hand in a rhythmic motion 10 times or so. Your left hand does not stimulate.
    5 Stop and hold without rocking the leg for 30 seconds.

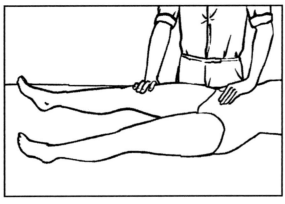

Fig.15

42

MANIPULATION 17: WRIST FLIP

The wrist flip is a passive mobilisation technique. This simple movement promotes relaxation and better energy flow through the wrist joint. The air and ether contacts (forefinger and thumb) create a diagonal flow of energy through the wrist which helps to stimulate the deep flow of energy in this joint.

Step 1 Stand at client's right side.
    2 With both hands grasp her right wrist. Your thumbs(ether) are on top of the wrist and your air (index) fingers are underneath the wrist (Fig. 16).
    3 With your little fingers (earth) flip the wrist in an upward motion 10 times.
    4 Hold the wrist without flipping for 15 seconds and feel for energy.

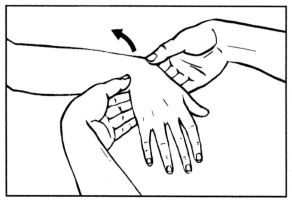

Fig.16

MANIPULATION 18: ARM AND SHOULDER ROTATIONS

This manipulation stimulates the energy currents flowing over the arms and shoulders. This is another very relaxing technique, this time influencing wrist, elbow and shoulder simultaneously and encouraging joint mobility. This technique is usually a good indicator of how willing the client is to let go and relinquish control in their lives. Many times you will find the client doing this rotation for you and finding it impossible to release one or all of the joints in question.

Step 1 Stand at client's right side.

2 From holding the client's right wrist as in the previous manipulation slide your thumb and forefingers down on to the hand.

3 Then using her hand to control the movements, rotate her arm in a relaxed circular motion (towards you). Do this movement 10 times in one direction and then 10 times in the opposite direction (away from you). (Fig. 17).

4 Your arms and hand should always be relaxed. This will help the client relax.

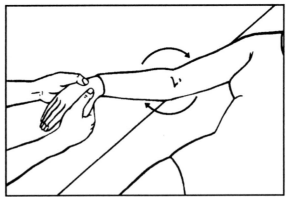

Fig.17

MANIPULATION 19: FINGER AND ARM STRETCHES

The purpose of these manipulations is to free the energy currents in the fingers. the technique is similar to the toe pulls and tendons compression, except that instead of working on the negative poles of the feet we are influencing the neuter pole of the hands. Once again it influences all five elements as the energy flows through the long energy lines of the arm and hands.

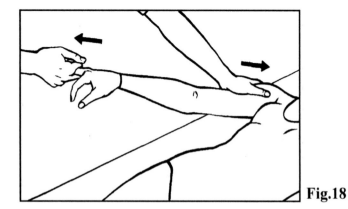

Fig.18

Step 1 Stand at client's right side.

    2 Grasp client's right thumb in between the air and fire fingers of your right hand. Hold her thumb as close to its base as possible.

    3 Holding the thumb firmly (without squeezing it), stretch her arm towards you, making it taut.

    4 With your left hand grasp her wrist and push away from you as you simultaneously pull the finger towards you. BE gentle, do not over stretch the arm.

    5 Repeat step 3 at the elbow and then at the shoulder (Fig. 18).

    6 Repeat steps 1-4 on each finger of client's right hand.

MANIPULATION 20: THUMB AND WEB CONTACT

This manipulation stimulates all the reflexes in the palm that relate to the organs beneath the diaphragm*. The right hand thumb and web contact will influence the liver and gall bladder, whilst the left hand contact will influence the stomach and spleen thus having a positive effect on the whole digestive system.

Ref: Hand reflexes, appendix Chart F

Step 1 Stand at client's right side.
     2 Place the side of your left thumb alongside the mound of Venus of client's right hand (Fig. 19).
     3 Place the tip of your index (air) finger in the web between her thumb and air finger on the back of her hand.
     4 Stimulate both points by pressing your fingers together. This point is usually very tender on most people. Remember not to use force.
     5 Stimulate for 1-2 minutes.

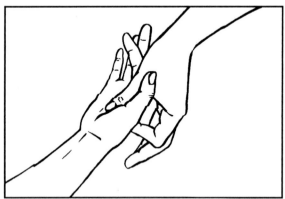
Fig.19

MANIPULATION 21: THUMB AND WEB CONTACT WITH INSIDE-ELBOW REFLEX POINT

In this manipulation two reflexes are being worked together. It combines the hand reflexes to all the organs beneath the diaphragm with a reflex point on the inside of the elbow. As we work these two points we are affecting mainly the fire and earth elements which are very active in the digestive region. Very often you will hear the organs in question gurgling in response to the stimulation of the reflexes.

In this manipulation and the next we are using alternate stimulation with only one reflex being stimulated at a time. This creates a *push-pull* effect on the energy flow.

Step 1 Stand at client's right side.
    2 Repeat steps 1 and 2 of Manipulation 20.
    3 With the thumb of your right hand contact a point on client's right forearm. Locate this point by finding the bony spot on the inside of her right elbow. From there move down 1 inch and then in 1 inch (Fig. 20). This is a liver reflex point. (On the left arm it is a stomach reflex point)
    4 Alternately stimulate the thumb and web contact, with a circular stimulating movement on the forearm 4 – 5 times.

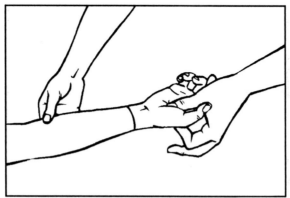

Fig.20

MANIPULATION 22: ELBOW AND LOWER-RIB CONTACT

This manipulation works by combining the digestive/abdominal reflexes that are located around the elbow with a direct contact over the organs themselves.

Step 1 Stand at client's right side.

2 Hold client's right elbow in the palm of your left hand. Place your left thumb on the forearm just below her elbow.

3 Place your right hand on her abdomen just below the diaphragm, so that her lower ribs fit between your thumb and air fingers. Your fingers should be pointed towards her left side (Fig. 21).

4 Stimulate the elbow by pressing first down and then up towards her shoulder. It should be a smooth circular movement.

5 Alternate the elbow stimulation with a gentle rocking of the abdomen. Alternately stimulate each place 4-5 times.

6 Continue for 2 minutes and then hold without stimulation.

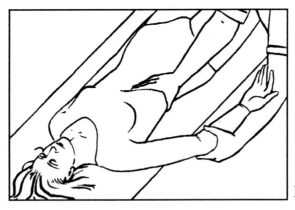

Fig.21

MANIPULATION 23: PELVIC ROCK

This manipulation stimulates the deep caduceus currents. It is also an activation of the five-pointed star energy pattern*. It affects all of the organs lying on a diagonal line between the two hands. As it is a diagonal contact it brings into play the caduceus currents, which in turn will influence the five lower chakras. It is also an effective release for the shoulders and hips and when performed with a stretch at the end of the movement as this encourages the front of the body to open up to release the diaphragm. At this point the client will often take a deep breath.

Ref: Five Pointed Star, page 150

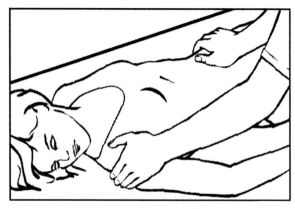

Fig.22

Step 1 Stand at client's right side.
    2 Place heel of your right hand on the inside of client's left pelvic bone (Poupart's ligament or inguinal ligament).
    3 Place the heel of your left hand on the front joint of her right shoulder. The fingers of your left hand gently grasp her right shoulder (Fig. 22).
    4 Press down on the shoulder as you rock her pelvis 10 – 15 times. Start gently and gradually increase the rocking movement. Remember, don't use any force.

MANIPULATIONS 24 – 30

Repeat manipulations 16 – 23 on client's left side. Remember to substitute right hand for left, etc. After completing the left side of the body, this would be the time to do any specific manipulations found in this chapter. If you are not doing any specific manipulations, continue with the general session.

MANIPULATION 31: ORBITAL CORNER AND OCCIPITAL RIDGE

This helps to balance the energy currents on each side of the head. This manipulation illustrates the principal of working on a specific current line of energy, in this case it is the ether current line. The ether line will tend to influence all the organs that lie close to the central axis of the body. It is also a good release for the eyes.

Step 1 Sit at client's head.
    2 Place your right fire finger on her occipital ridge. The point is 1/2 inch to the right of the spine.
    3 Place your left air finger on the point between her nose and right eyebrow.
    4 Hold the nose/eyebrow point (orbital corner). With the fire finger of your right hand gently stimulate the occipital ridge (Fig. 23).
    5 Stimulate for 1 minute and then hold for 30 seconds. Feel for tingling.

Fig.23

MANIPULATION 32

Same as Manipulation 31. The only difference is that you do it on client's left side. Make sure to reverse the hands.

MANIPULATION 33: CRANIAL BALANCE

The Cranial balance, (sometimes known as the spider), is a lateral balancing technique in which each on the ten fingers tend to influence the corresponding current lines as they flow over the head. The anterior fontanel is a powerful point for creating balance in the body. We can also tune into the energy in each of the current lines, which makes this hold a valuable technique for assessing the efficacy of our treatment. This is a satvic hold which will encourage integration and resonate with the core energy.

Step 1 Sit at client's head.
    2 Place both your thumbs in her front fontanel.
    3 Place your little (earth fingers on the jaw points on either side of her head. This is in front of the ears and can be felt when client opens and closes her mouth (Fig. 24).
    4 Place your other fingers wherever they fall naturally. They should be symmetrical on both sides of the head.
    5 Hold for 1-2 minutes and feel for the energy.

Fig.24

MANIPULATION 34: SENSORY/MOTOR CURRENTS BALANCE

This manipulation will balance the energy currents on the front of the body with those on the back. This is a sensory/motor balance. The raised claw shape of the left hand will draw off any excess prana that may have built up around the head during the treatment. A slight traction can be applied to the forehead thereby creating a release of the frontal bone of the skull. This technique is also a satvic hold.

Step 1 Sit at client's head.
    2 With your right hand grasp client's neck and slide your hand up until you hook
    3 her occipital ridge with your thumb and air fingers (see Manipulation 2). Place the thumb of your left hand on her front fontanel.
    4 The other fingers of your left hand make a claw shape as you place your fire and water fingers on either side of the nose (Fig. 25 and 25a).
    5 Hold for 1 minute and feel for energy.

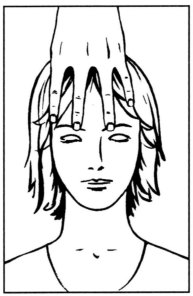

Fig.25

Fig.25a

MANIPULATION 35: UMBILICAL BALANCE

Finally, the fiery life centre in the umbilicus is balanced with the third eye of the head. It balances the fire element and the fire principle and is a satvic hold.

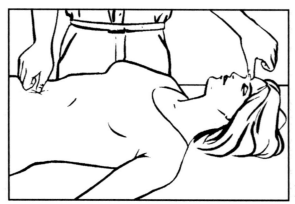

Fig.26

Step 1 Stand at client's right side.
 2 Make loose fists with your hands and place your right thumb in her navel.
 3 Place your left thumb at the point between her eyebrows (Fig. 26).
 4 Hold for 2 minutes and feel the life energy.

MANIPULATION 36: BACK BRUSHING

These last two techniques of the General Energy Balancing Session, balance the energy on the surface of the body by connecting the therapist's positive hand to the negative side of the clients body and the negative hand to the positive side. As the hands are moved down the body all of the energy is balanced and any excess will be pushed downwards where it is grounded or absorbed into the greater energy field of the planet. This is a good way to complete any session as it alleviates any possible feeling of being light headed or spaced out.

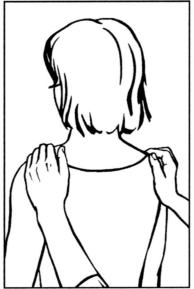

Fig.27

Step 1 Stand behind client.
    2 Place your hands on her shoulders.
    3 Bring your hands toward one another and cross them at her spine and neck. Then brush the body down on either side of the spine to her buttocks (Fig. 27).
    4 When you have reached the buttocks, uncross your hands and repeat steps one to three, 5 to 10 times. The brushing is done as a gentle continuous movement. Try doing the last 2-3 brushes 1/2 inch from the body. See if you can feel her energy.

MANIPULATION 37: FRONT BRUSHING

Client is seated, hands on her thighs or knees.

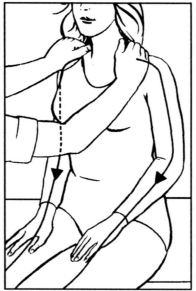

Fig.28

Step 1 Stand in front of client.
    2 Place your hands on her shoulders, alongside her neck (Fig. 28).
    3 Brush your hands in one continuous motion out to her shoulders, down her arms and her legs.
    4 Repeat 5-10 times. Do the last 2 brushes 1/2 inch from her body.
    5 If it feels right, this is a great time for a big hug.

Please note that the suggested number of times or minutes to stimulate or hold are approximate. Time available, intuition and experience will be your best guides. The general treatment can take from 20 – 45 minutes with equal effectiveness. Experiment and enjoy.

BALANCING THE THREE DIVISIONS OF THE NERVOUS SYSTEM

This session promotes relaxation by balancing energy in the cerebro-spinal, parasympathetic and sympathetic divisions of the nervous system.

In the upper contact the fingers affect the para-sympathetic nerve reflex area along the top line of the shoulders, whilst the palm covers the sympathetic nervous system reflexes on either side of the spine as well as the spinal cord itself which reflexes into the cerebro-spinal system directly. The lower contact also affects all three systems, the palm over the buttock line affects the lateral para-sympathetic nerve reflexes which are an extension of the perineal floor, and the finger tips influence the perineal/coccygeal area where the para-sympathetic and sympathetic systems terminate. The pelvis as a whole is the negative pole of the central nervous system.

By using diagonal contacts on the body we stimulate the deep caduceus currents. This manipulation is very relaxing and is most beneficial at the end of a Polarity session. When followed by the next two manipulations, 90 per cent of my clients fall asleep. A relaxed client is the sign of a good Polarity session. In a relaxed state the life energy flows better and life energy is the power that heals.

Client is on her front.

Step 1 Stand at client's left side.

2 Place your left hand so that it contacts the area where her neck and shoulder meet on her right side. A portion of the palm of your left hand should be across her spine (Fig.29).

3 With your right index (air) finger locate the end of her coccyx. This is the tailbone at the end of her spine between the buttocks. After touching the end of the coccyx, move your air finger a quarter of an inch below it. The rest of your fingers and hand will cover the lower left buttock.

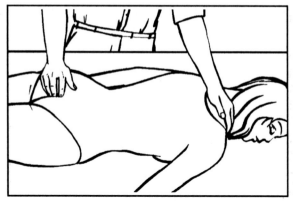

Fig.29

4 Rock her left buttock for several minutes while holding the shoulder contact without stimulation.

5 Repeat this manipulation on her right side. Remember to change hands.

CHAKRA BALANCE

The chakras are powerful centres of whirling energy located at different areas of the spine. Each of the five physical chakras gives rise to one of the five currents of energy associated with each of the five elements. These centres of energy are also related to the organs and functions of the body in the areas they are located (see Fig. 3, p. 10).

The first part of this treatment involves drawing the five elements into the spine by placing the right hand palm up over the earth chakra. The palm up position is a essentially the same hand mudra that is used in Oriental meditation practice to draw in energy from the cosmos. The hand rotation over the chakra is used to encourage it to spin freely. The four lower chakras are balanced in relation to their supply chakra, the ether chakra, and then the ether and third eye chakra are balanced with the crown chakra. All contacts follow the basic law of Polarity, as the left hand is kept higher on the body whilst working on the neutral central axis where the chakras lie. As you balance the chakra system you will also be balancing the five elemental energies and the endocrine system as the major glands of this system lie in the vicinity of the chakras. It is also possible to do a chakra balance on the front of the body. In the session the earth and water chakras are treated together as one contact however it is quite possible to make a contact over the coccyx area for the earth chakra and then another separate contact over the lumbo-sacral junction for the water chakra. An effective way to finish this session is to place the left hand over the crown and place the right hand on the coccyx and wait until you feel the energy moving smoothly and strongly between the two hands.

Note: Stimulating a toe or finger with one hand while placing your other hand over the centre or chakra related to it is an effective way to stimulate that area of the body.

Client is on her front.
  Step 1 Stand on her left side.
      2 Place your left hand on the back of her neck (ether chakra).
      3 Place your right hand palm up over the sacrum (water chakra) and coccyx (earth chakra). Your fire or middle finger is in line with her spine and your fingers are pointed towards her head (Fig. 30).
      4 With your right hand stimulate the lower chakras with a circular clockwise movement for 2 minutes. Your left hand does not stimulate.

Hold and feel energy. This palm position attracts the five elements from cosmos into the spine. (Fig.30)

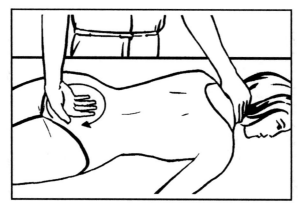

Fig.30

5 Now place your right hand palm down over the same area. Rotate your right hand 90 degrees to the right (Fig. 31).

6 Stimulate this area with a clockwise circular movement for 1 minute. Your left hand remains on the neck with no stimulation.

7 Repeat steps 5 and 6 over the fire chakra (opposite her solar plexus) and then over the air chakra (between her shoulder blades). Stimulate each place for 1 to 2 minutes and feel for the energy as warmth or tingling.

8 Now move your right hand to her neck and place your left air finger on the third eye chakra (between the eyebrows). Hold for 2 minutes without stimulation.

9 Now place your left hand on the crown chakra (over the front Fontanel) and hold for 2 minutes.

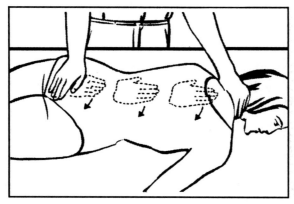

Fig.31

BALANCING RESPIRATORY, EMOTIONAL AND SENSORY CURRENTS

This session helps to relieve mental, emotional and nervous tension and is probably the most calming and relaxing one in the book. The technique balances the chakras as well as the para-sympathetic nervous system and is a good release for the diaphragm.

It uses sensory contacts (a very light touch) on the back on the body, the motor area, to induce a profound polarity balance and deep relaxation. The contacts influence all of the five bi-lateral current lines. The contact points are along the top line of the shoulders, which is the positive pole of the diaphragm, the air astrological triad and the para-sympathetic nervous system reflex area and the lower contact is along the lower line of the buttocks, which is the negative pole of the diaphragm as well as being lateral para-sympathetic nerve reflex areas, on the same line as the perineal floor. This treatment can be made more effective by encouraging the client to breathe deeply during the session to facilitate the release of deeply held emotional energy.

Client is on her front.

Step 1 Stand at her left side.

   2 Points of contact are on the top of the shoulders and on the bottom line of the buttocks.

   3 Contacts are done simultaneously and are non-stimulating. The shoulder contact is with either your air or water finger of your left hand (negative contact). The buttock contact is with your right fire finger (positive contact). The contact points are marked with x's (Fig. 32).

   4 Place your left air finger on the edge of the left shoulder. With your right fire finger, contact the left buttock line so that it is approximately in line with the shoulder contact.

   5 Move your fingers away from you inch by inch until you reach the edge of the right shoulder and right buttock. Hold each contact until you feel energy flow. (Fig. 32).

6 Then make diagonal contacts. Place your left air finger on the edge of the right shoulder. With your right fire finger, contact the edge of the left buttock line.

7 Move your contacts inch by inch in opposite directions. Your left hand moves back towards you as your lower right hand move away from you.

8 Cover client with a sheet or blanket and let her relax for several minutes or more. Many clients are asleep at this point.

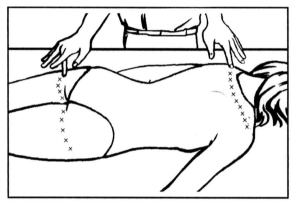

Fig.32

The following are points to remember:

a. Your fingers do not touch one another.

b. The contacts are made as lightly as possible.

c. Have client breathe deeply but in a relaxed way during the treatment. This helps distribute life energy through the breath to the entire body.

BALANCING THE ETHERIC AND CAUSAL BODY ENERGY CURRENTS

According to Dr Stone, man is triune. He has a physical body, an etheric body and a causal body. The etheric and causal bodies consist of finer and more vibratory energies. The causal body contains the blue print for the etheric and physical bodies. Working with the life energy in these more subtle bodies affects those of a lower vibration.

During this treatment I have found it best for the recipient to not talk and keep her eyes closed. For those who meditate it is useful to repeat their mantra mentally. One may also just concentrate on observing the breath. These techniques help the receiver to reach deeper states of emotional calm and physical relaxation. Seeing colours and lights and feeling energy are common experiences for those receiving this treatment.

For the practitioner the most important aspect of this treatment is your relaxation and your concentration on feeling for energy as you contact the body. Hold each of the body parts or chakras gently with your entire hand. The palm of your hand should be over the centre of each part when possible. This treatment can also be done with your hands one to two inches above the body. Experiment and see what feels best.

It is helpful to visualise energy flowing into your medulla oblongata (at the base of your skull) and down into your hands and into your client. You may enhance the effects by concentrating your attention at the point between your eyebrows (the 3rd eye) and/or by mentally chanting "OM". Hold all contacts for 2 minutes or until you feel the energy equally in both hands.

This treatment releases physical and emotional energy blocks and as the name implies, resonates strongly with the more etheric quality of life energy. There is no stimulation in the session - just satvic holds. It also balances the chakra system and is deeply relaxing and integrating. It can be most beneficial in highly nervous cases where a calming session is required. The initial contacts are on the major joints in the body which are neutrally charged areas, which resonate strongly with the ether element. The second set of contacts are directly on the chakras (both on the spinal axis and to the side). The term "causal body energy" relates to the chakra system. In many metaphysical explanations of the nature of reality, the chakras are the basis of the causal layer of reality - the blueprint or level of causation of experience both physically and mentally.

Don't cross your hands or stimulate, and when making the contacts gently mould your hands to her body.

Client is on her back.
Stand behind client and make the following contacts:
Left and right shoulder
Move to her right side
Right shoulder and right side of waist
Waist and right hip
Right hip and right knee
Right knee - right ankle
Tops of both feet
Move to her left side
Left ankle - left knee
Left knee - left hip
Left hip - right hip
Left hip - left side of waist
Waist - left shoulder
Place your right hand over the navel. The left hand will be placed over each of the major chakras. Remember to hold each contact for 2 minutes or until energy is felt equally in both hands - CONCENTRATE! Hold the chakras in the following order:
Pubic bone
2 inches below the navel or between the pelvic bones
Now change sides and continue. (Your right hand remains over the navel.)
Spleen - Below the diaphragm and floating ribs on the left side of the body.
Solar plexus - just below the sternum
Heart. Centre of the chest
Throat
Forehead
Crown (front fontanel)
12-18 inches above the crown, palm facing the head.

It usually takes 20 minutes or so and can be combined with a good, general balancing session. *Note:* This session can be performed just off the body which makes it even more etheric in nature but be advised that some clients may find the lack of contact disconcerting.

GAS RELEASING TECHNIQUES

These techniques are designed to locate and free gases trapped in pockets in the body. Gases created by poor digestion can diffuse through the body and become trapped virtually anywhere, causing a great deal of discomfort. Recurrent pains in the arms and legs can be caused by gases trapped in the Haversian canals of the bones. Headaches are often caused by gases trapped in the cranium (or sometimes by reflex action caused by gas problems lower down in the digestive tract).

The gas releasing techniques are a treatment of the air principle in the body; the lungs being the positive pole (the intake of air), the colon is the neuter pole (a gas reservoir) and the calves of the legs are the negative pole. In yogic and ayurvedic philosophy the air principle is composed of five different qualities of prana, sometimes referred to as "the five vital airs" or "Vayu's." There are five different directions of movement of the Vayu's. In this treatment "Udana," the third of the vital airs is being affected. Udana is situated in the region of the diaphragm. It governs upward movement in the body such as expiration, coughing, belching, speech and vomiting. The fifth of the vital airs, "Apana," is also being influenced. Apana, which is located in the large intestine, governs the downward movement in the body and expels gases and solids from the bowels.

The effect of the various manipulations is fairly obvious, but note that the second one is a seated diaphragm release. It would seem, that these techniques, are more physical manipulations than energetic. However, remember that all matter is a reflection of energy so any coarse gases that are released as a result of these techniques are indications of the release of the subtle vibrations of life energy also. All techniques should include a gentle hold and sensing for the release of the life energy at the end of each manipulation.

Remember it is no good just treating the gas problem without looking at what caused it in the first place. Dietary change may be applicable as well as specific bodywork for any digestive system imbalance and emotional holding.

GAS RELEASING MANIPULATION 1

Client is seated

Step 1 Stand behind client.

    2 Place your hands on top of the iliac crests on both sides (Fig. 33). With your fingers in front and your thumbs behind knead her abdomen in the area of the cecum on the right and the sigmoid on the left (see colon, Fig. 89, p. 128).

If she belches or you hear gurgling sounds, the gases are being released. Stop kneading until these responses stop. Do each manipulation in this treatment until you hear a response or until client feels relief. Patience is the key in this treatment.

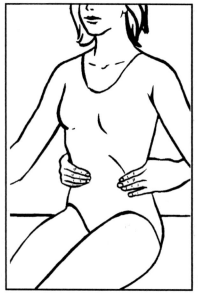

Fig.33

GAS RELEASING   MANIPULATION 2

Client is seated

Step 1 Remain behind client.

    2 Place the fingers of your left hand under the diaphragm on her left side close to the centre (sternum).

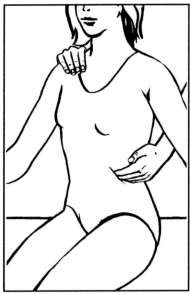

Fig.34

3 Place your right hand on her right shoulder. Your right thumb is on her back alongside the upper dorsal or thoracic vertebrae (Fig. 34).

4 Simultaneously push her shoulder forward as you lift under her diaphragm with the fingers of your left hand.

5 Move along the diaphragm back and forth from the sternum to the floating ribs looking for gas pockets. Hold if belching or gurgling occurs.

6 Switch hand and repeat steps 1 - 4 on the opposite shoulder and opposite side of the diaphragm.

GAS RELEASING MANIPULATION 3 - BRACHIAL PLEXUS

This manipulation is the same as the manipulation described in the Brachial Plexus Release (see p. 109).

Client is seated.

Step 1 Stand behind client.

2 Place her left hand behind her back.

3 Place your left hand on the front of her shoulder.

4 Place the fingers of your right hand under the bottom portion of her shoulder blade (scapula). Your elbow is resting on your right knee (Fig. 35).
5 With your left hand on front of her shoulder, pull the shoulder back towards you so that your fingers slip behind her shoulder blade.

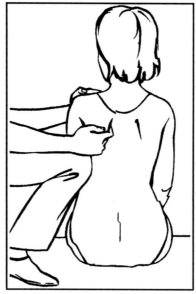

Fig.35

6 Lift your right hand to release her shoulder blade (brachial plexus) by raising your knee. At the same time lift her shoulder with your left hand. Hold for a few moments and lower. Repeat several times.
7 Then move your hand a little higher and repeat the previous procedure. Continue as high on the scapula as you can.
8 Repeat on the opposite shoulder blade and shoulder. (Switch hands and knees).

If you cannot get your fingers under the shoulder blades do the first manipulation of the diaphragm release. This is the negative lock to the brachial plexus. Stimulating between the big toe and first toe is effective as well. The brachial plexus release is excellent for any breathing difficulties, low energy, heart trouble, digestion and shoulder pain.

GAS RELEASING MANIPULATION 4

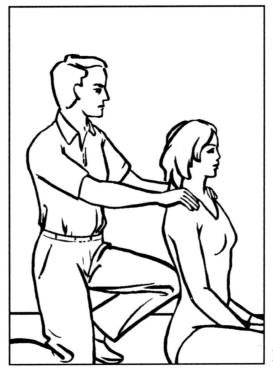

Fig.36

Client is seated.

Step 1 Kneel behind client.

    2 Place your hands on top of her shoulders with your fingers above the clavicles (collar bones).

    3 Place your left knee along the left side of her spine near its base (Fig. 36).

    4 Squeeze her shoulder muscles as you pull her back into your knee which acts as a fulcrum.

    5 Move your knee up and down her back looking for gas pockets. Hold when belching occurs.

    6 Repeat steps 1-5 with your right knee on the right side of her spine.

GAS RELEASING MANIPULATION 5

Client is seated.

Step 1 Stand behind client.

2 With your right fire finger do a deep rotating massage in the groove next to her spine on the right side. Start close to the shoulders and work up to the occipital ridge. Repeat 3-4 times or until you hear the gases release (Fig. 37).

3 Switch hands and do the left side of her neck.

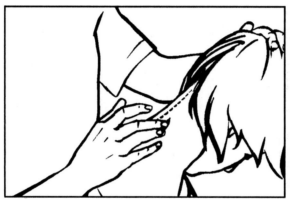

Fig.37

GAS RELEASING MANIPULATION 6

Fig.38

Client is on her back.

Step 1 Stand behind her.

2 Overlap your hands on her neck just below her occipital ridge. Your thumbs are on the jaw (Fig. 38).

3 Tilt her head forward.

4 Gently stretch her neck by pulling it towards you. Rock her gently forwards and backwards as you pull and stretch it. Repeat 3 - 4 times.

The sitting position favours the movement of gases upwards. For people with gas problems, nutrition is obviously important. Eating too fast, improper food combining, overeating and eating foods high in sulphur are possible causes. A bland diet of pureed foods along with the Polarity purifying diet is very beneficial.

CONTACTING THE FIERY LIFE CENTRE IN THE UMBILICUS

The following series of manipulations affect the embryonic energy pattern. This vital energy flows as radiating waves from the centre (umbilicus) outwards (see Chapter 1). It is through these contacts that the primal energies of Yin and Yang, which wove the body together in the womb (the fundamental spiritual involutionary energy) can be influenced.

There is a difference of opinion as to the relationship of the navel to the fire chakra. The umbilical energy centre (nabhi) is not synonymous with the fire (Manipura) chakra. The fire chakra is part of the caduceus system, the source of whose energy is the prana in the atmosphere drawn in via the breath. Its location physically is close to the solar plexus.

The umbilical centre draws in a vibration of fiery cosmic prana that is unavailable through the breath. This energy relates to the soul as the vital spark from the creative flame, the primary involutionary impulse. Prebirth, *all* the energies that we need, both cosmic and earthly are drawn in via the navel connection to the mother. Post birth, the chakra system works with the physical breath to draw in the earthly prana from the atmosphere, whereas the umbilical centre continues to draw in the cosmic prana. The chakra/caduceus is an inactive seed potential until the baby is born and the first breath taken yet the umbilical centre is fully active from conception when there is no physical breath and continues to act separately from the breath throughout the rest of an individual's life.

It is also through the umbilicus that we receive the energetic patterning from our ancestors, especially our immediate parents. It is this patterning that forms our basic constitutional energetic imprint. If we are blessed with a good constitution, due to good influences whilst we were forming in the womb, then we generally have good, robust health throughout our lives. If our constitution is poor then illness and disease can plague us throughout our life. If you have a weak constitution it is best to live a moderate life style that puts as little stress on your being as possible.

Client is on her back.

Step 1 Place the thumb of your right hand in her navel.

2 Sink it down and in the direction of the energy block.

3 With the fingers of your left hand stimulate gently in the direction of your thumb. Fig. 39 shows a contact over the liver area with the left hand.

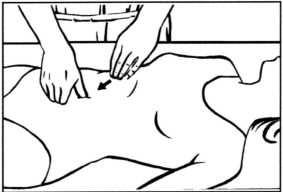

Fig.39

4 Stimulate for several minutes or until the tenderness disappears. Try this manipulation on yourself. Your left hand can be placed anywhere on the body (pelvis, chest, joints, abdomen, arms, legs or head).

Note: Either thumb may be used as they are neutral in Polarity and can be combined with any other contact. (See Law of Polarity, p. 14). Thumbs are also very effective at pushing energy. The navel contact is first downward into the navel and then the thumb is turned towards the other hand in the direction in which you want the energy to flow.

UMBILICAL CONTACTS COMBINED WITH VARIOUS REFLEXES FOR THE FOLLOWING

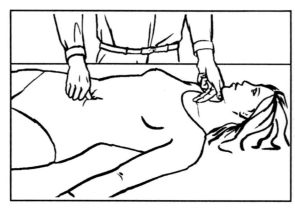

Fig.40

THYROID	Opposite hand lifts under the clavical with air and fire fingers. Do both sides. Hold for two minutes on each side (Fig. 40).
CHEST PAIN	(Angina Pectoris) Opposite thumb gently stimulates sore areas on the left shoulder contact (contact B, Fig.41)
LIVER / GALL BLADDER	Opposite hand over third, forth and fifth ribs on the right hand side and then use your thumb on sore spots above right elbow and knee contacts (contacts C, D, E Fig.41)
STOMACH	Same as liver but on the left side (contact F, G, H, Fig.41)
KIDNEYS	opposite hand or thumb on sore spots on outside of each ankle (contact I, Fig.41)

Treat any sore spot on the body; these always indicate blocked energy. Use light contacts *without force*.

SENSORY CURRENT RELEASE

This manipulation is very beneficial in promoting a profound state of relaxation and is very soothing for nervous people and for relaxing irritated and over-stimulated areas on the body. It releases the sensory spiral currents of energy.

Client is on her back.

Step 1 Place right thumb in navel. Combine the thumb contact in the umbilicus with each of the other contact areas in the order listed.

The thumb contact in the navel exerts a light pressure directed downwards and toward the opposite hand which will be gently stimulating various areas in turn. After gently stimulating each area for 30 seconds, hold gently, close your eyes and concentrate deeply on feeling a tingling sensation where your hand is in contact with the body. Remember to keep the thumb contact directional at all times. Use all your finger tips on each of the other contact areas where possible. Contacts are very, very light. This manipulation is excellent practice for sensing energy.

2 *Stand on client's right side.* Right thumb in navel and left hand on right jaw (in front of ear). Then, in sequence, stimulate the following areas:

Right front shoulder joint
Right inside elbow joint
Front of right wrist
Palm of right hand at navel area (see Fig. 106)
Right hip joint
Top of right knee
Top of right ankle
Sole of right foot at navel area (see Fig. 106)
(Fig. 41, anterior view, illustrates all contacts with small dotted circles.)

Note: You may change thumb and hand contacts as needed for comfort. Remember not to cross your hands.

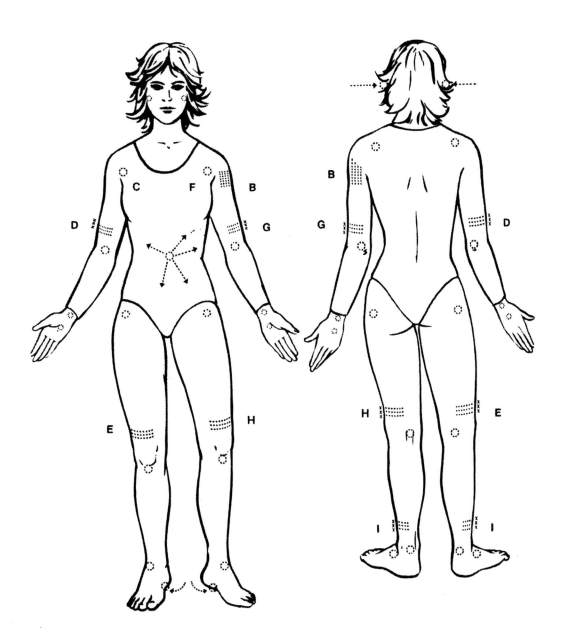

Fig.41

3 *Now switch sides.* Keeping the thumb contact in the navel make the following contacts in sequence.

   Sole of left foot at navel area
   Top of left ankle
   Front of left knee
   Left hip joint
   Left palm at navel
   Front left wrist
   Inside left elbow
   Front left shoulder
   Left jaw joint
   (Fig. 41, anterior view, illustrates all contacts with small dotted circles.)

4 Put the right thumb in navel, left thumb on Third Eye chakra (See Fig. 26, Chakra Balance.)

MOTOR CURRENT RELEASE

Improves circulation, lymphatic drainage and releases the posterior motor spiral currents of energy.

   Client is on her front.
Step 1 Place right thumb on the spine opposite the navel, a point between the second and third lumbar vertebrae. There are five lumbar vertebrae. The fifth is just above the base of the sacrum. Moving up the spine count backwards and place your thumb between the second and third lumbar (Fig. 42).

   2 Combine this directional contact with a contact on each of the seven major joints. This releases the motor currents. Include the navel area on the top of the foot and the back of the hand (Fig. 41, posterior view). A firm and rhythmic stimulation (no force), is used on all the contact areas. Stimulate each area for 30 seconds or so, stop and 'feel' for the energy.

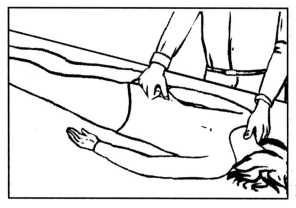

Fig.42

In sequence, the contact areas are as follows:

Left jaw
Left shoulder
Left elbow
Left wrist
Back of left hand
Left hip
Left knee
Back of left ankle
Top of left foot

Now switch sides.

Top of right foot
Back of right ankle
Right knee
Right hip
Back of right hand
Right wrist
Right elbow
Right shoulder
Right jaw

Note: You may change thumb and hand contacts as needed for comfort. Remember not to cross your hands.

PERINEAL TREATMENT

In addition to being one of the most profoundly relaxing treatments, perineal work can be combined with a variety of contacts to effectively unblock energy anywhere in the body. It is very useful for chronic neck and shoulder tension, nervousness, emotional blocks, stress, sciatica, low back pain, lumbago, leg pain, during pregnancy, thyroid problems, etc.

The perineum or perineal muscles are the most negative pole (lowest point) on the torso at the base of the pelvis. These muscles attach to the ischium bones which are the bones we sit on and can be felt on both sides near the crack in the buttocks. Releasing the tense perineal muscles produces a relaxing effect on its positive pole in the neck and upper torso. This area is also the negative pole of the para-sympathetic nervous system and so the perineal treatment activates this branch of the autonomic nervous system helping to increase relaxation and improve digestion.

The perineal area is the gateway to the deep energy currents that flow down the legs and treatment here is indicated in all leg conditions. It is also a way of influencing the deeper muscles of the pelvis to re-establish equilibrium and to aid posture and balance of the organs and muscles of the pelvis. It is invaluable in back conditions especially where there is pain on movement.

Mind and its thoughts are energy and its blocks are as real as those in the body. The perineal treatment correctly done deals with the vital force of emotional energy. It is interesting to speculate on the meaning of the phrase "the seat of the emotions." How many times when you are upset have you sat on your emotions to control them? As we literally sit on our perineal floor it seems there is some real significance to that phrase and a fundamental truth expressed by calling the perineal treatment, "Mental and Emotional Therapy".

Finally, it is important to note that the perineum is the lowest point at which we can influence the ultrasonic core energy.

It is clear from the above why a good perineal treatment can create the biggest change in the energy fields of any single Polarity treatment.

Currents flowing to and from the perineum (caduceus currents) cross over the spine so you only need to treat one side although it is fine to do both.

It is important to establish, through Practice on different perineal floors, whether the muscles are too tight or too flaccid and vary your technique accordingly. Generally if the perennial muscle is very tense then hold firm steady pressure until the muscle relaxes; if the muscles seem loose and flaccid then more vibratory and stimulating contacts are used.

Ref: Perineal contacts, appendix Charts G & H

To fully balance the relationship between the nervous and circulatory systems when doing the perineal technique, if the pulse felt at the carotid artery is fast stimulate the area around the first, second and third cervical vertebrae lightly with the thumb and air finger of the left-hand, whilst holding the perineal floor with the fire finger of the right hand. If the pulse is slow then hold firm steady pressure on the neck area and the perineal floor until the pulse normalises.

Client is on her left side. Place a pillow under the head for comfort. Knees are well bent, at least 90°.

Step 1 Stand or sit behind client.

    2 With fire finger of right hand working through a tissue contact area 1. This is found where the ischium bone and pubic bone meet. All contacts are next to the ischium bone. Feel for it and use it as a guide. Slide your fire finger below and alongside it. (Fig. 43).

       The thumb and fingers of the left hand are placed on the neck on the sides of the spine just below the occipital ridge (Fig. 44).

    3 Hold the neck.

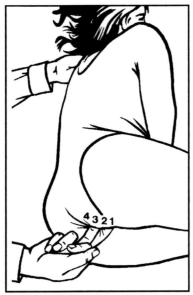

Fig.43

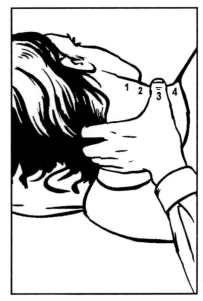

Fig.44

    4 With the fire finger on the perineum, starting with gentle pressure, direct or lift the finger towards the head or neck. If it is sore hold it until it relaxes and then increase the depth of the contact slowly until the soreness disappears and/or you feel the energy.

    5 Continue the same procedure on areas 2, 3, 4 on both the perineum and the neck.

    6 The fire finger goes as deep as possible without force as the muscles relax.

    7 You may repeat the above on the opposite side. Remember to switch hands.

VARIATIONS

1 Contact any sore point on the perineum with your fire finger. With the opposite hand hold or stimulate any sore points in the areas listed below:

The region of elbows and/or knees	For digestive disorders
Inside and outside of heels	For pelvic disorders
Hip, shoulder	For diaphragm and jaw problems

Client is on her front. Place a firm pillow under the pelvis to raise it.

2 Use all four fingers of the hand (excluding the thumb) on the entire perineum, or with the fire finger on the sorest point. Lift towards the head. Combine this with any of the following contacts using your thumb, when possible, or all of the fingers:

Buttocks	For pain and muscle tension in the pelvic area
Achilles tendon	For low back pain
Spinal muscles	For tension in the back (Fig. 45)
Top of shoulders	For diaphragm release
Heel reflexes	For prostate, uterus, bladder problems (Fig. 46)
Kidneys	For circulatory problems

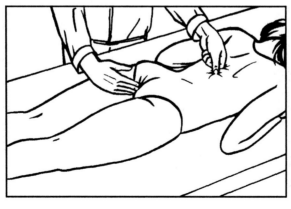

Fig.45

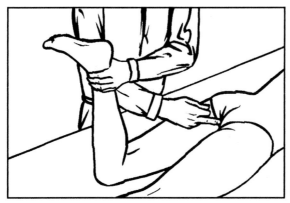

Fig.46

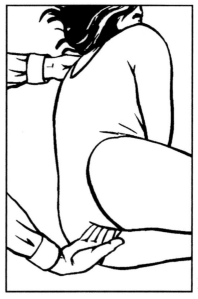

Fig.47

Client lies on her side.

3 Use all the fingers on the perineum at once. With the other hand stimulate sore spots as designated in variation 1 (Fig. 47).

4 Hold any area on perineum with corresponding neck area for 5-10 minutes.

5 Be creative - experiment - the perineum can be combined with contacts virtually anywhere. Remember, use no force. Go as deeply as client's body will allow.

RELEASING NECK TENSION

These three techniques release blocked energy in the neck manifesting as pain or tension and are different ways of working on the ether element and ether oval field. Manipulation 1 and 2 use the fingertips and opposite Polarity of contacts to release blocked energy. The first uses an anterior-posterior (sensory - motor) release straight through the body, the second uses diagonal contacts through the centre and so activates the deep spiralling caduceus currents of energy in the ether oval. The third manipulation polarises with a diagonal contact on the next oval field above to release the energy blocks. Polarising blocks to areas in one oval field with the related areas in the oval field immediately above or below is a very effective treatment principle.

RELEASING NECK TENSION 1

Client is on her back.

Step 1 Sit at her head.

2 With the fire finger of your right hand reach as low down on the right side of her neck as you can. Contact a point close to the spine (Fig. 48).

Fig.48

3 Press with your fire finger. If the spot is sore draw an imaginary diagonal line through the centre of her neck from your fire finger, to a spot on the front of her neck on the opposite side. Contact this spot with your left air finger. It should be sore.

4 Alternately stimulate both places very gently until the soreness disappears or energy flows.

5 Continue along the right side of her neck by moving your fire finger up towards the occipital bone.

6 For each sore spot you find repeat step 3 above.

7 When you reach the occipital ridge, switch hands and do the other side of her neck (steps 2-6).

RELEASING NECK TENSION 2

This treatment is especially beneficial for sore throat, tonsils, thyroid and laryngitis.

Client is on her back.

Step 1 Sit at her head.

2 With your left air finger find a sore spot in the throat area. Start between the clavicles and work towards you.

3 For each sore spot you find on the front, find a corresponding sore spot with your fire finger on the vertebra opposite your air finger (Fig. 49).

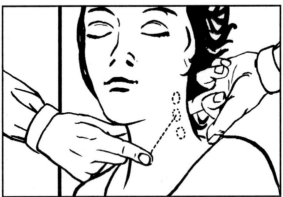

Fig.49

4 Alternately stimulate both contacts for 30 seconds. Stop and feel for energy. Check for soreness. Repeat, if necessary. Remember to stimulate gently.

5 Move to another spot. Treat each sore spot the same way.

RELEASING NECK TENSION 3

This session releases blocked energy along the sides of the neck, and helps to restore rotational ability in the neck muscles.

Client is on her back.

Step 1 Stand alongside the side of the neck you are treating.
   2 With the thumb of the lower hand, locate sore spots on the side of the neck.
   3 For each sore spot, place your thumb against it. The fingers of that hand are under the neck, out of the way.
   4 Place the other hand on the opposite side of the head (forehead area), Fig. 5.

Fig.50

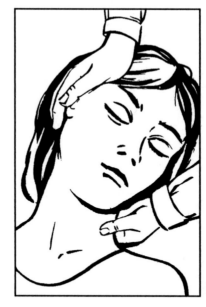

Fig.51

   5 Using your thumb on the sore spot as a fulcrum, slowly turn the head into your thumb. Be gentle.
   6 When you feel resistance, stop relax your hands and then continue until the head has turned as far as it can go (Fig.51).

ETHERIC CURRENT TREATMENT

The treatment is, in essence, running the energy through a particular current line to clear blockages anywhere along it. The ether currents are the long currents of energy closest to the centre of the body. They pass through the thumbs and the big toes. Stimulating this current treats everything that the currents pass through. The etheric current treatment is effective for stimulating and balancing the activity of the endocrine system and for such conditions as thyroid deficiency or over activity because the ether current line runs close to the central line of the body and most of the endocrine glands are themselves close to the centre of the body. It also passes over many important organs such as the uterus, prostate and heart and helps with problems in these areas too. It can very effective in the treatment of menstrual problems and cystitis. The session will also influence the ether chakra as the current lines form a communication link with their source. It can therefore be valuable in opening the ether field for more free emotional expression and release. You can of course contact more points along the current line than those illustrated if you so wish or deem necessary to get a full flow through the current line.

This treatment principle can be used on any of the five bi-lateral current lines. All you need to do is adjust the hand positions to interact with the appropriate current line. For example, to run the energy through the earth current line all the contact points are moved out from their positions near the centre line (where they are on the ether current line) to points along the outside edge of the body on the earth current line.

MANIPULATION 1: AT THE NEGATIVE POLE OF THE FEET

Client is on her back throughout this treatment.

Step 1 Stand at client's feet.

2 Grasp the big toe of her right foot between the air and fire finger of your right hand (Fig. 52).

3 On the inside of her big toe next to the corner of the nail find a sensitive or sore spot by pressing down firmly with the side of your thumb.
4 With the air finger of your left hand find a sore spot somewhere on the inside of her right heel.

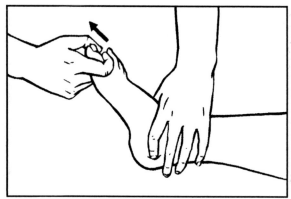

Fig.52

5 Alternately stimulate these two points for 1 - 2 minutes or until the tenderness disappears. Feel for energy.
6 Repeat this manipulation on her left foot. Remember to switch hands in the instructions.

MANIPULATION 2: AT THE NEUTER POLE OF THE HANDS

1 Stand at her side.
2 Repeat the exact procedure that was done on her big toe (Fig. 52) on her thumb. The base of the thumb at the wrist corresponds to the inside of her heel.
3 Find a tender spot on the inside corner of her thumb near the nail and contact a tender spot on the base of her thumb with your air finger. Alternately stimulate for 1-2 minutes. Hold for 30 seconds and feel for energy.
4 Repeat this procedure on her left thumb.

MANIPULATION 3: FOR ENDOCRINE GLANDS, STOMACH AND HEART

Step 1 *Stand at client's right side.*

    2 With your left air finger between her clavicle bone, gently hook under the one nearest you and find a tender spot. This treats the thyroid gland (Fig. 53).

    3 With the fire finger of your right hand find a tense or sensitive spot half an inch or so down from the sternum in your direction. It may be on the diaphragm or below it. This treats the pancreas (Fig. 53).

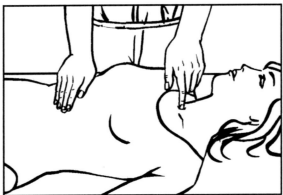

Fig.53

    4 Alternately stimulate these two points for 2 minutes or until tenderness disappears. Hold and feel for energy flowing.

    5 Keep your right fire finger on the diaphragm area. With your left air finger locate a sensitive spot on her right eyebrow about half an inch from her nose (pineal gland).

    6 Alternately stimulate these two points as in step 4 above.

    7 Keep the right fire finger on the diaphragm and move your left air finger to her occipital ridge. Locate a sensitive spot half an inch or so from the centre of the occipital ridge on the side nearest you (pituitary gland).

    8 Alternately stimulate as in step 4 above.

9 Keep your air finger on her occipital ridge. Ask her to bend her knee so you can grasp her Achilles tendon which is located just above the heel on the back of her leg. Grasp the tendon with your thumb and the side of your air finger. Find a sore spot (Fig. 54).

10 Alternately stimulate for 2 minutes. Hold and feel for the flow of life energy.

11 Repeat steps 2 - 10 on the left side of client. In addition to the endocrine glands, this side benefits the stomach and the heart. Remember that sensitive, tender or painful spots alert you to the energy blocks. Always look for one of these spots to stimulate. Always stimulate gently without any force.

As blocked energy is released the soreness usually disappears or lessens considerably. If it does not, stimulate for an additional minute, hold for 30 seconds and move on.

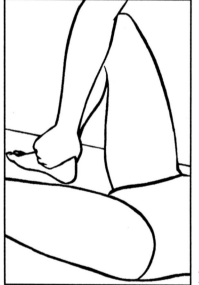

Fig.54

MANIPULATION 4: FOR THE PELVIC AND REPRODUCTIVE ORGANS

(uterus, ovaries, bladder, prostate, penis and testes)

Step 1 Stand at client's right side.

2 With your thumb on top and your fire finger on the underside, gently grasp her pubic bone (look for tender spot) half an inch or so from the centre of her body on your side (Fig. 55).

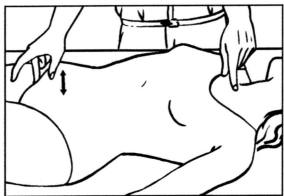

Fig.55

3 With your left air finger locate a tender spot on the opposite side of her body between the clavicle bone and the rib just below it half an inch from the centre of her body. Cross over the body to involve the deeper caduceus or serpentine currents which cross over the spine (Fig. 55).

4 Alternately stimulate the pubic bone and the spot between the clavicle and first rib gently for 2 minutes. Hold and feel for energy.

5 Maintain the pubic bone contact and move your left air finger to the spot next to her nose and eyebrow, also on her left side.

6 Hold this point without stimulation and stimulate the pubic bone for 2 minutes.

7 Move your left air finger to the occipital ridge on her opposite (left) side, and find a tender spot half an inch or so from the centre. Alternately stimulate the occipital ridge and the pubic bone.

8 Now release the contact on the pubic bone. Have client bend her right knee and contact her Achilles tendon with the thumb and air finger of your right hand.

9 Alternately stimulate the Achilles tendon and the occipital ridge for 2 minutes. Hold and feel the life energy flow (Fig. 56).

10 Repeat steps 2 - 9 on client's left side.

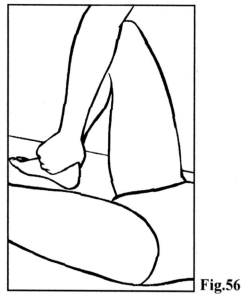

Fig.56

TREATING BLOCKED ENERGY IN THE SHOULDER

This session frees energy in the shoulder manifesting as pain or soreness. The first of the four manipulations in this treatment is a manipulation of the five-pointed star (see page 150). The technique releases the base of the star in the lower pelvis, which in turn frees the energy currents to the shoulder on the opposite side. The second manipulation is a release of the five current lines at the neuter pole of the diaphragm and positive pole of the shoulders. The third manipulation (brachial plexus release) relaxes all of the deep musculature in the motor area of the shoulders. As a treatment format for shoulder pain this works both the front and back of the body. Working the front has a powerful effect on the back, and vice versa, through the tri-axial geometry of the body i.e., front/back, left/right, top/bottom.

MANIPULATION 1

Client is on her back.

Step 1 Stand on the side opposite the sore shoulder.

    2 Place the fingertips of both hands on the inside of the pelvic bone on your side (Poupart's ligament).

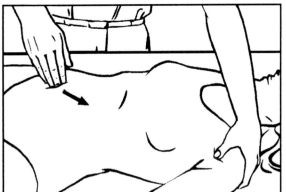

Fig. 57

#109 02-14-2012 3:24PM
Item(s) checked out to ESHLER, PAMELA FR

TITLE: Hands-on healing : a practical gu
DUE DATE: 02-28-12

Martin Library
Sunday Hours 1-5pm

3 Slowly and gently work along the shape of the pelvic bone. Press down and towards the sore shoulder. Hold until you feel the muscles relax. Then go deeper. Remember not to use force.

4 Now remove your top hand and grip the sore shoulder with your thumb in the shoulder joint (Fig. 57).

5 Alternately stimulate the pelvis and shoulder until you feel the energy move.

MANIPULATION 2

Do Manipulation 3 of the diaphragm release on the sore shoulder side (see Fig. 71).

MANIPULATION 3

Do a Brachial Plexus Release on the sore shoulder (see p. 109).

ADDITIONAL MANIPULATIONS

You may also use the reflexes in the feet and the hands prior to doing the above manipulations (see p. 145-148)

KIDNEY TREATMENT

This is a treatment for the kidney energy. It utilises stimulation of the kidney reflex points in the feet. In the first part of the first manipulation your thumb is on the kidney area of the foot whilst the fingers of the same hand rest around the ankle. The other hand, which is pumping the foot, is resting on the ball of the foot which is a reflex to the upper chest. As you flex the ball of the foot and ankle you are in effect stimulating all three poles of the air astrological triad (shoulders, kidneys, ankles) by indirect or reflex action. The second part of the first manipulation stimulates the kidney reflex in conjunction with reflexes to the whole middle section of the body, front and back The second manipulation connects the kidney reflex to the actual organ, (an important stage in all Polarity reflex work), and the third manipulation connects an air reflex point near the ankle to the kidney itself. This treatment is, of course, indicated in all problems of the kidneys, high blood pressure and in periods of acute and chronic stress where the adrenals are put under pressure. It would be beneficial to finish the treatment with a balancing of the air triad. This can be accomplished by connecting the ankles to the kidneys, then the kidneys to the shoulder and finally the shoulders to the ankles on both sides of the body. Hold and feel for energy at each place.

Ref: Foot Reflex, appendix Chart F and p. 146

MANIPULATION 1

Client is on her front

Step 1 Stand at her left side near her foot.

2 Lift her left foot by bending her knee.

3 Place your left thumb on the kidney reflex on the sole of the foot (Fig. 58). See foot reflex chart, Fig 105.

4 Flex the foot with your right hand to bring the blocked energy closer to the surface of the foot. With the foot flexed firmly stimulate the kidney area with your thumb. It should be sore or tender.

5 After 1 minute or so, grasp the foot with your right hand so that it is in line with your left thumb. Flex the foot and stimulate the kidney area with your thumb (Fig. 59) for 2 minutes.

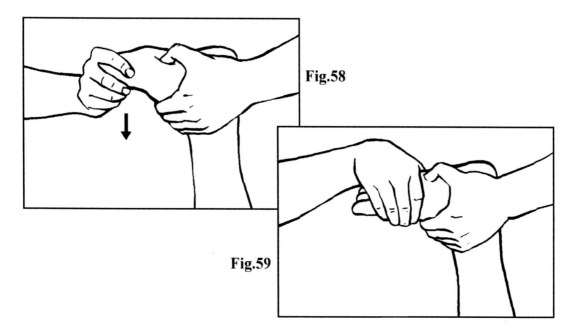

Fig.58

Fig.59

MANIPULATION 2

Client is on her front.

Step 1 Place your right thumb on the kidney area of the foot (see Fig. 105) and place the heel of your left hand over her left kidney. This is found alongside the lower dorsal vertebrae (11th and 12th). It is usually sore.

2 Alternate stimulation on the foot and the kidney until the soreness lessens (Fig. 60). Then hold and feel the energy.

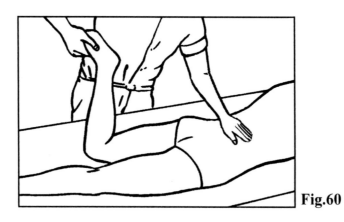

Fig.60

MANIPULATION 3

Client is on her front.

Step 1 Keep your left hand on the kidney.

2 With your right thumb contact the lower leg area on the outside of her left leg above the heel. Find a sore point.

3 Firmly stimulate the leg area while holding the kidney area without stimulation.

4 Continue stimulating until the soreness in the calf disappears. Then hold without stimulation for 30 seconds (Fig. 61).

Repeat Manipulations 1, 2, 3 and 4 on her right side.

Note: The kidney on the right side is a little lower in its position due to the size of the liver.

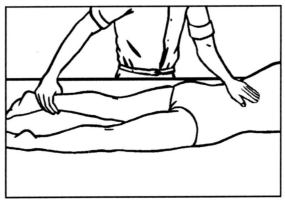

Fig.61

FOOT REFLEX TREATMENT

The same principles and method with slight variation can be used to treat the energy in any organ of the body. The foot reflexes connected to the corresponding body areas is the method employed. The long currents of energy flowing over the body are stimulated and balanced. The kidney treatment is an excellent example of this principle. For most organs of the body, the client will be on her side or back so you can reach the front of her body. The kidneys, however, are located close to the back of the body and so in the previous session client is on her front. Most internal organs are located closer to the front of the body.

Step 1   Look carefully at Fig. 105, p. 146. Note that the toe areas reflex to the head and the heel areas reflex to the pelvis. In addition, note that the sole of the right foot reflexes to the front right side of the body and that the sole of the left foot reflexes to the front left side of the body. This chart will give you a general sense of where the various body organs are and where the corresponding foot reflexes are located.

    2   Place the person you are working on in a position which facilitates bi-polar contacts. Lying on the back or side usually works when stimulating organs close to the front of the body or on the front for treating blocked energy on the back or the kidneys. This is because the tops of the feet reflex to the back of the body and the soles to the front.

    3   Flex the foot containing the reflex you want to stimulate with one hand. Place the thumb of the other hand on the reflex with the rest of your fingers opposite it on the top of the foot. Massage the reflex with your thumb for 2-3 minutes.

    4   Move the hand which is flexing the foot so that it grips the sides of the foot in line with the reflex. Continue to massage the reflex for 2-3 minutes more.

    5   Now with one thumb stimulate the reflex. With the fingers of the other hand alternately stimulate the area of the body related to the reflex.

The tops of the feet reflex to the back of the body. The soles of the feet reflex to the front.

THE FIRE OF DIGESTION

This session is useful in order to stimulate the digestion and is beneficial for colds and for the eyes. The treatment uses the air toes and air fingers as reflexes to stimulate the air element as it passes through the digestive area of the body. It uses triune function by stimulating the jaw which is a positive pole to the neuter digestive region. The air toes are stimulated rather than the fire toes because stimulating air makes the fire hotter for better and more complete digestion.

This session is essentially a treatment of the air element through the air current lines. Most digestive troubles are not due to problems with the stomach, liver and intestines per se, but with the fact that the fiery fluids of digestion are stuck in their reservoirs (e.g., bile in the gall bladder) and are unable to get out. The cause of this is an energy block in the air element due to emotional stresses which divert the impulse to movement. The gall bladder, for instance, is seen as the reservoir for jealousy, bitterness, hatred and resentment and releasing the energy that flows through this organ will help to release these negative emotions as well as improving digestive function.

The air fingers and toes are stimulated so as to get the fluids moving by means of a general stimulation of the air element. The gallbladder itself lies approximately on the air current line on the right side of the body and the first joint of the right air finger and toe is a specific reflex to it. The jaw contact point in this session is another reflex to the gallbladder and duodenum.

The treatment is beneficial in eye trouble and headaches, particularly when such problems are due to gas pressure from poorly digested, fermenting food. The eyes are the positive pole of the fire element and will benefit from the overall improvement in the functioning of the fire element, but the air current line also passes through the pupil of the eye and so this is another factor. Specific indicators for this treatment are headaches, pulling and straining sensations behind the eyes, gas pains, abdominal cramps, feelings of discomfort after eating, excessive belching, neck and shoulder pain and, of course, gall bladder problems.

MANIPULATION 1

Client is on her back throughout this treatment.

Step 1 Stand at her feet.

    2 With your thumb and air fingers grasp her air toes on either side at the first toe joint (Fig. 62). Simultaneously squeeze and pull each toe towards you and hold for one minute. The right toe reflexes to the gall-bladder; gall-bladder duct and part of the duodenum and the left toe to the duodenum as well. Remember that soreness means blocked energy.

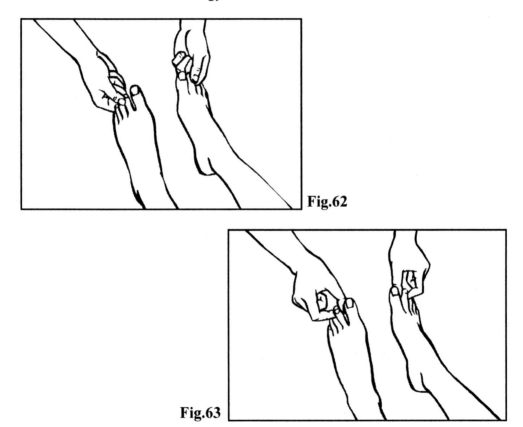

Fig.62

Fig.63

    3 After one minute grasp the same air toe with your thumb and air fingers (Fig. 63) but on the top and bottom of the first joint. Squeeze and pull for 1 minute.

    4 Alternate steps 3 and 4 until soreness lessens or disappears.

MANIPULATION 2

Stand at client's right side.
Repeat Manipulation 1 (toes: negative pole) on the air fingers (neuter pole) (Figs. 64 and 65).

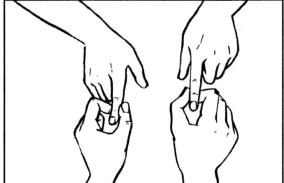

Fig.64

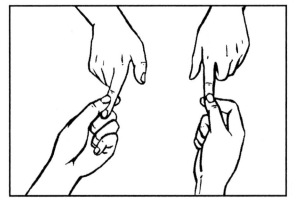

Fig.65

MANIPULATION 3

Step 1 Stand at the right side of client's head.
    2 Place your left hand on top of her head (Fig. 66).
    3 Your right thumb contacts her right jaw on a point that is directly in line with the centre of her right eye. The fingers of your right hand are under the jaw.
    4 Stimulate and/or hold for one to two minutes and feel for energy.
    5 Keep your left hand on top of her head and move your right thumb and fingers to her left jaw in line with the centre of her left eye. Stimulate or hold for one to two minutes and feel the energy.

Fig.66

MANIPULATION 4

This is exactly the same as Manipulation 3, except that you stand at her left side and reverse your hands. Your right hand is on top of her head and your left thumb and fingers are on the jaw contact points. The jaw point on the right side is the positive pole to the gall-bladder, gall-bladder duct and duodenum and the jaw point of the left side is the positive pole to the duodenum (beginning of the small intestine). The right hand on top of her head stimulates the long currents flowing down the body. The left hand on top of her head stimulates the long currents flowing up the body (the right hand being positive pushes energy and the left hand being negative receives energy).

MANIPULATION 5

Step 1 Stand at the side of client's right leg.

    2 Grasp her right air toe at the first joint with your right thumb and air finger (Fig. 67).

    3 Place the fingers of your left hand over the area of the gall-bladder duct and duodenum on her right side. This area is approximately 1 inch above and 2 inches to the side of her navel nearest you (Fig. 67).

Step 4 Alternately stimulate these two points until you feel energy move (a warm or tingling sensation).

    5 Now combine the air toe contact with a similar contact on her right air finger.

    6 Alternately stimulate these points. Feel for energy.

    7 Now combine the contact on her air finger with the contact used in step 3. Alternately stimulate the finger and abdomen. Feel for energy.

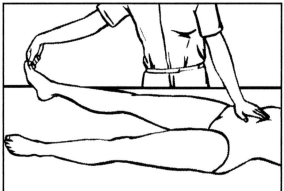

Fig.67

MANIPULATION 6

Repeat Manipulation 5 of this Fire of Digestion treatment on client's left side. Remember to switch hands on the contacts.

MANIPULATION 7: ROCKING NECK STRETCH

This is the same manipulation as Manipulation 6 of the Gas Releasing Manipulations.

Fig.68

Note: This entire Fire of Digestion treatment can be done using client's fire toes and fire fingers instead of the air toes and fingers. The difference would be that the right fire toe and finger are reflexed to the liver and the left fire toe and finger are reflexed to the stomach. The jaw and abdomen contacts are moved slightly to the outside of the client's body. This puts the contacts in line with the fire current flowing through the fire toes and fingers.

This variation is excellent for the stomach and liver and is good for digestion. In this case the fire element is being treated directly to improve its function.

DIAPHRAGM RELEASE

This session frees blocked energy in the diaphragm for improved breathing, better digestion and more energy.

The major release point for the diaphragm is found in its most negative pole. This is under the big toe (ether) joints on the bottom of each foot. Remember that it is always most beneficial to release the negative pole first. These are found in the feet or pelvis. This will benefit the flow of energy in the neuter and positive poles.

The diaphragm is a uniquely important muscle in Polarity as it is the major neuter pole in the body in that it separates the top from the bottom in terms of the tri-axial geometry of the body. Its freedom of movement is essential to physical and emotional health. It is also an important fulcrum in the energy pattern of the five-pointed star.

The first manipulation is on the foot reflexes to the diaphragm. Your air finger hooks under the ball of the foot to contact one diaphragm reflex whilst the thumb works between the big toe and its neighbour to reflex to the brachial plexus in the upper back and so too to the diaphragm (as one of its positive motor poles).

The second part of the treatment uses the tibia release point on the top of the ankle (see ankle manipulation in general session) and connects it to the diaphragm.

The third manipulation works along straight line currents at the clavicle line, which is the positive pole of the diaphragm and connects them to related points over diaphragm.

The fourth is a technique that stimulates the five-pointed star at the shoulder and along the diaphragm.

MANIPULATION 1: BIG TOE JOINT RELEASE

Client is on her back.

Step 1 Stand at client's feet.

2 Grasp her right big toe by hooking the big toe joint with the side of your right air finger. Your thumb is placed on top of her foot opposite your air finger (Fig. 69).

3 Stimulate the big toe joint by sliding the side of your air finger back and forth for 1-2 minutes. Then hold for 30 seconds and feel for energy.

Note: This same point will help blocked sinuses and also free the brachial plexus which is located behind the shoulder blades. (see p.109)

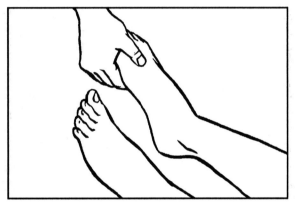

Fig.69

MANIPULATION 2: TIBIA RELEASE POINT AND DIAPHRAGM

Client is on her back.

Step 1 Stand alongside her right leg.

2 Place your right thumb in the hollow spot on top of her right ankle. This is called the tibia release point and is the same point stimulated in Manipulation six of the general treatment. Your other fingers are on the outside of her leg.

3 Place the fingers of your left hand under the diaphragm muscle (Fig. 70).

4 Move along the diaphragm inch by inch from the centre (sternum) to the outside (floating ribs). You are looking for tense or tender areas.

Fig.70

Step 5 For each tense, tight or tender spot on the diaphragm, stimulate the tibia release point by rocking her leg with your right hand. As you push her leg away from you, press on the tibia release point with your thumb. Let her leg return to the starting position by itself. Alternate the leg rocking with stimulating the sore spot on the diaphragm. Gently and rhythmically stimulate both contacts five to six times each until the diaphragm relaxes.

MANIPULATION 3: CLAVICLE AND DIAPHRAGM CONTACTS

Client is on her back.

Step 1 Stand at client's right side.

2 With your left air finger locate tender spots 1 inch below her collar bone (clavicle). Start at the centre of her body and work towards you. This is the positive pole to the diaphragm (Fig. 71).

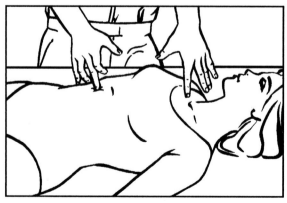

Fig.71

Step 3 For each tender spot you find under the clavicle bone, place your right fire finger in a direct line with your left air finger on the diaphragm itself (Fig. 71). Find a tense or tender spot on the diaphragm.

4 Alternately stimulate both points until the tenderness under the clavicle disappears or until you feel the energy flowing.

These three manipulations are done by stimulating the long currents of energy flowing vertically over the body (see Fig. 1). Repeat these manipulations on client's left side. Remember to change hands. Another way to free blocked energy in the diaphragm is by stimulating the deep caduceus currents which cross over the spine (Fig. 3). This is done by using the following manipulation:

MANIPULATION 4

Client is on her back.

Step 1 Stand at client's right side.

2 Grasp her left shoulder with your left hand. Place your left thumb in the front joint of her shoulder.

3 The fingers or thumb of your right hand will go under the diaphragm of her left side (Fig. 72).

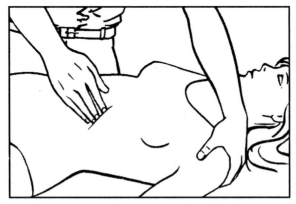

Fig.72

Step 4 Move along the diaphragm inch by inch. At each spot on the diaphragm you will lift her shoulder towards your right hand as you press under the diaphragm in the direction of her left shoulder.

5 Firmly stimulate the shoulder joint with your thumb as you alternately stimulate tense areas on the diaphragm. Repeat until the diaphragm relaxes or energy is felt. Then hold without stimulation for 30 seconds.

MANIPULATION 5

This is done with your left hand on client's right shoulder and your right hand on her diaphragm on the right side of her body. Repeat steps 1- 4 of the preceding manipulation (Fig. 73).

Note: Having the palm of your right hand turned up makes for a more relaxed contact.

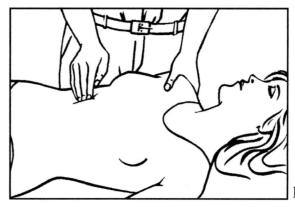

Fig.73

BRACHIAL PLEXUS RELEASE

The brachial plexus technique is designed to release energy blocks underneath the scapula that are adversely affecting the nerve plexus that lies in this area. It can be most helpful in painful conditions of the neck, shoulders and arms and to aid in breathing problems such as asthma.

The cervical nerves from which the brachial plexus is formed are linked by rami communicantes to that part of the sympathetic nervous system that forms the cardiac plexus which controls the heart and lungs. It is an important technique for releasing energy blocks that are affecting the heart, which in Polarity terms is where the air, fire and water elements are mixed. The shoulders are the positive pole of the air element and the brachial plexus is the motor pole of the air element in its respiratory and cardiac functions. In general the more sick the person is, the tighter the shoulder blades. The actual point to release is about one inch below the top of the scapula. In all cases of chronic illness or pain this is an important area to release. The scapulae are sometimes referred to as "the wings of life."

If it is difficult to get under the scapula go to the negative pole at the feet and work the first manipulation in the diaphragm release treatment. (see p.105) Five minutes of work here will greatly facilitate the work on the scapula.

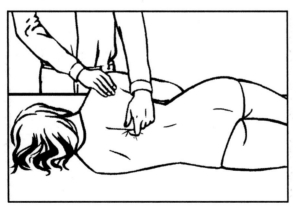

Fig.74

In addition to performing the technique with the client her on her side (Fig 74), it may be done with her in a seated position. The seated variation is Gas Releasing Manipulation 3 (see p. 66). It may also be performed with the client lying on her back.

The idea in all variations is to get your fingers under the scapulae (shoulder blades) and with a lifting motion free the brachial plexus.

CRANIAL BALANCE (HEAD TREATMENT)

To balance and stimulate life energy flowing through the head and cranial bones. This is an excellent treatment for relaxing tension in the facial muscles and cranial bones. It is beneficial to those people who have overactive or restless minds as the light etheric quality of the touch encourages restfulness or sleep by spacing out the "fire" energy in the head. It is a good release for the jaw and cranial bones and is helpful in sinus problems.

The head is the positive pole of the whole of the body and contains reflexes to the entire body, as do the feet, so doing the treatment benefits all the body. This technique uses the air fingers as a negative pole when making the contacts on the positive head to create a balance. It is a lateral balancing technique.

Client is on her back.

Step 1   Sit at her head. With the air fingers of both hands, make simultaneous, symmetrical contacts on both sides of the head on the following bones.

    2   The jaw (Fig. 75). Start in the centre of the chin and work out half an inch by half an inch along the jaw to the ears (contact A). Gently stimulate each pair of contacts alternately until energy flows.

    3   Then move to the jaw joint in front of the ear. From here move in towards the nose along the bony ridge below the eyes (Fig. 75, contact B).

    4   Start next to the nose and eyebrow and work out along the orbital bones (eyebrow area) toward the ears (Fig. 75, contact C).

    5   From the ears go along the top of the forehead to the centre of the head (Fig. 75, contact D).

    6   Then, with your fingers 1 inch apart, go along the top of the head all the way over to the occipital bone at the base of the skull (Fig. 76, contact E).

    7   With the air fingers move along the occipital ridge half an inch at a time to the temporal bone behind the ears. (Fig. 76, contact F).

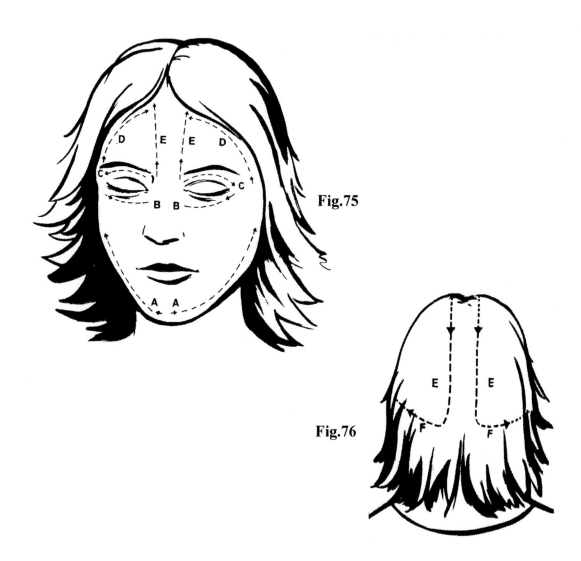

Fig.75

Fig.76

Points to remember

1 Make symmetrical contacts, fingers to be on the same spots on both sides of the head.

2 Gently stimulate alternately on each pair of bones for 15 - 30 seconds. Stop, feel for energy and then continue. Move the fingers half an inch at a time along the cranial bones.

PELVIC RELEASE

This session helps to free blocked energy in the pelvis. It is excellent for releasing emotional blocks and for promoting relaxation. The treatment releases specific sore areas in the pelvis by using the left and right hands as positive and negative holds to push the energy through the blocked areas. The energy release principle expressed in this simple treatment can be used to good effect anywhere on the body. Think of this as a pin point energy release technique because the fingertips allow for a very precise release of small areas of blocked energy. The technique described predominantly influences the water element by making front and back contacts on the water oval field.

Client is on her front.

Step 1 Sit at her left side.

  2 Mentally divide her left buttock into 5 vertical lines or zones.

  3 With your left fire finger go down each vertical line inch by inch. Press firmly looking for tender spots (energy blocks).

  4 For each tender spot you find have client raise her pelvis and place your left hand underneath. With your right fire finger locate a tender spot directly opposite the tender spot on the buttock (Fig. 77).

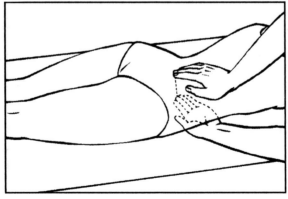

Fig.77

Step 5 Very gently with your fire fingers on the tender spots and all your fingers together to give you the power of the entire hand, alternately stimulate several times. Then hold and feel for the energy. Repeat until the tenderness disappears or the energy flows.

6 Repeat the above procedure on the right buttock.

Note: A cleared pelvis (no energy blocks) will make any manipulations which combine foot reflexes and body contacts more effective, e.g. kidney treatment as energy must flow through the pelvis from the feet in order to reach the rest of body.

LYMPHATIC TREATMENT

This session is designed to stimulate the flow of life energy in the lymphatic system of the body and is beneficial for colds and swollen glands.

The lymphatic system contains 45 pints of lymph fluid. One of the functions of this fluid is to bathe the cells of the body and remove cellular toxins. It is a vital eliminative system of the body.

The treatment stimulates the water element in its function as the lymphatic system in the body. The techniques are done on the major areas of concentration of lymph nodes. It uses a rhythmic squeezing to stimulate the flow of lymph and energy.

The umbilical centre is used because of its fiery involutionary quality, which aids in fighting infection, stimulates activity in the lymph system generally and aids in the elimination of toxins. The active fiery energy of the umbilicus is also used to stimulate and move the water element which is a passive element. There are also major lymph nodes in the area of the navel.

In many ways the lymphatic system is the forgotten system in the body, and is only now receiving the kind of attention hitherto reserved for the other major systems such as the cardiovascular, respiratory, digestive and nervous systems.

This treatment is best combined with other cleansing practices such as skin brushing, breathing exercises and Epsom salt baths. Daily exercise such as walking aids in lymphatic flow.

MANIPULATION 1

Client is on her back.

Step 1 Stand at client's right side.

 2 Place your right thumb in her navel. The thumb should press down and in the direction of her right shoulder.

 3 Stimulate the right side of her neck and the top of her right shoulder. Do this by squeezing your fingers and the heel of your left hand together. Start at the neck and move downwards towards the shoulder (Fig. 78).

Step 4 Repeat step 3, five to six times while holding the navel contact. Then hold both contacts without stimulation for 30 seconds. Turning your client's head to her left will make stimulation of the neck and shoulder easier.

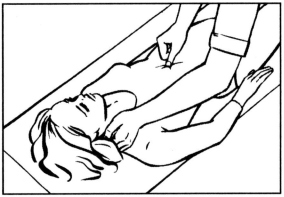

Fig.78

MANIPULATION 2

Client is on her back.

Step 1 Stand at her right side.

     2 Keep your right thumb in the navel as in the previous manipulation.

     3 Place your left thumb in her right armpit and with your fingers of your left hand stimulate her shoulder joint (Fig. 79) with a massage-type movement.

     4 Do this for 2 minutes.

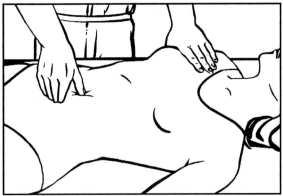

Fig.79

Step 5 With the right thumb still in the navel, continue the same massage-type movement at several points where the ribs attach to the sternum (between the breasts).

6 Go over this area between the breasts four to five times.

MANIPULATION 3

Client is on her back.

Step 1 Place both your hands on either side of client's right elbow on the inside of her arm.

2 Stimulate the inside of the arm with a squeezing motion.

3 Move your hands simultaneously, the left towards her shoulder and the right towards her wrist.

4 Repeat five to six times (See Manipulation 5 for a similar example, but on the leg).

MANIPULATION 4

Client is on her back.

Step 1 Stand at client's right side.

2 Place your left hand on the inside of her right pelvic bone (Poupart's ligament).

3 Your right hand will stimulate the inside of the thigh with a squeezing motion of the heel of your hand and your fingers (Fig. 80).

Fig.80

Step 4 Stimulate the pelvis gently with a rocking motion 3 - 4 times and alternately stimulate the inside of her thigh moving down towards her knee.

    5 Repeat this sequence 4 - 5 times.

MANIPULATION 5

Client is on her back

Step 1 Place both hands on the inside of the client's right leg, the left hand above the knee and the right hand below (Fig.81).

    2 Stimulate the inside of the leg with a squeezing motion of the heel of your hand and your fingers.

    3 Move your hands simultaneously. The right hand towards her ankle and the left towards her pelvis.

    4 Repeat 5-6 times.

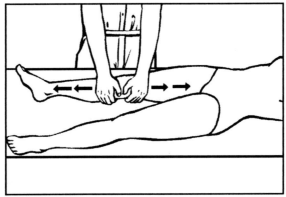

Fig.81

Client is on her front.

Step 1 Stand on her left side.

    2 In the area of the spine just below her neck, place your right hand on the right side of her spine and your left hand on the left side of her spine (Fig. 82).

    3 Stimulate by pushing away from you with the heel of your right hand and alternately pulling toward you with the fingers of your left hand. Continue this pushing and pulling movement down her spine to her buttocks.

    4 Repeat this procedure 4-5 times firmly but gently.

Repeat manipulations 1-5 on client's left side.

MANIPULATION 6

Client is on her front.
Step 1 Stand on her left side.
    2 In the area of the spine just below her neck, place your right hand on the right side of her spine and your left hand on the left side of her spine (Fig. 82).
    3 Stimulate by pushing away from you with the heel of your right hand and alternately pulling toward you with the fingers of your left hand. Continue this pushing and pulling movement down her spine to her buttocks.
    4 Repeat this procedure 4-5 times firmly but gently.

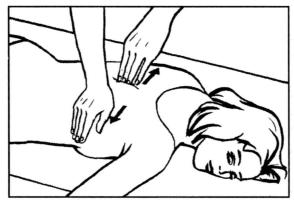

Fig.82

MANIPULATION 7

Client is on her front.
Step 1 Place the heel of your right hand on the bottom of her left buttock. Place your fingers on the buttock itself (Fig. 83).
    2 Place your left hand on top of her left shoulder.
    3 Stimulate the buttock by rocking it gently towards client's head several times.
    4 Alternately stimulate the shoulder with a gentle squeezing motion of your left hand several times.

119

Step 5 Repeat steps 4 and 5 several times.

Repeat this manipulation on client's right side.

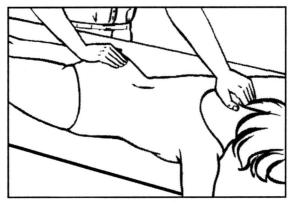

Fig.83

DRAINING THE UPPER LYMPHATICS

This treatment drains the upper lymphatic areas and stimulates energy currents in the neck and brachial-plexus area. It is good for head congestion, colds, sore throat etc. If so wished it can be incorporated into the previous lymphatic session between MANIPULATIONS 2 and 3.

Client is on her back.

Step 1 Stand on client's right side to treat client's left side.

    2 With your left hand grasp neck muscles.

    3 With your right hand grasp axillary muscles in the armpit area (Fig. 84).

    4 Using gentle squeezing movements, alternate rhythmically for one minute.

    5 Stop, hold and feel for the energy.

    6 Repeat for one minute.

    7 Change sides and repeat steps 1-6, changing hands as needed.

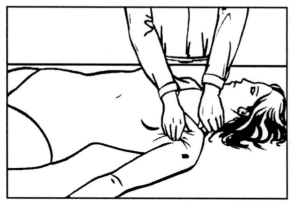

Fig.84

PROSTATE/UTERINE TREATMENT

The purpose of this session is to free energy in the prostate and uterus. The session begins with stimulating the ankle reflexes to the prostate/uterus and follows with a coccyx treatment and a perineal session. The perineal contact area can be anywhere from the symphysis pubis to about the midpoint of the perineal floor. The perineal treatment is used as a drainage release for the prostate/uterus.

Client is on her back.

Step 1 Stand at client's feet.

2 With your thumbs contact the sorest point below the inside ankle bone on both feet (Fig. 85).

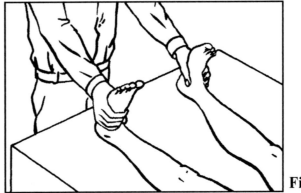

Fig.85

3 Hold for one minute. Then gently stimulate both points simultaneously for one minute.

4 Have client turn on her abdomen.

5 Do a coccyx treatment (p. 124).

6 Combine a perineal contact with your fire finger on point 2 (fig. 43, p. 80) lifting the finger gently upwards to help drain the prostate (for a man) or uterus (for a woman) with a thumb contact on the inside of the heel at the sorest reflex point. Hold for one minute. Relax for 30 seconds. Repeat for one minute.(Fig. 86)

7 Do this on both sides

Note: The foot reflexes to the prostate, bladder and uterus are all located close to each other on the inside of the heel below the ankle bone. Treat the sorest points first, using the above procedure.

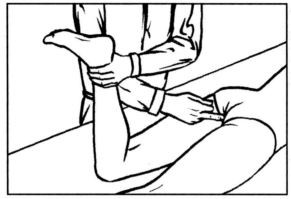

Fig.86

COCCYX TREATMENT

This treatment is used to free energy in the uterus, prostate gland, bladder and lower back. It is excellent for menstrual cramps. It can be invaluable when used for back problems where the pain is constant.

The treatment is a balancing of the sympathetic nervous system from its negative pole at the Ganglion of Impar, a nerve plexus which is situated on the anterior surface of the coccyx, with the cerebro-spinal function. The ganglion of impar is the end of the sympathetic nerve chain where it should polarise with the cerebro-spinal system. It is also a communication point between the right and left sides of the body. The technique affects the air, fire and water elements and also influences the earth chakra.

A simple balance to end this session would be contact at the coccyx with your right fire finger whilst gently holding the bridge of the nose with thumb and air finger of the left hand.

Client on her front.
Step 1 Stand on her left side.
     2 Contact will be made on the underside of the coccyx (tailbone) with your right fire finger. This spot is called the Ganglion of Impar.
     3 Spread the cheeks of her buttocks apart with the thumb and air fingers of your left hand.
     4 Move the skin of the buttocks towards her feet without actually moving your hand.
     5 Place a tissue over the coccyx area.
     6 With your right fire finger contact the underside of the coccyx through the tissue. Release your left hand.
     7 Contact the far side of the coccyx first. Do a gentle rotating type of stimulation (Fig.87).

8 Simultaneously stroke her right buttock with the thumb of your left hand. Stroke in the direction of her head (Fig. 87). The motion is a slow gliding one which distributes waste matter found as lumps or soreness in the muscles of the buttocks.

Simultaneously stimulate for 1 minute.

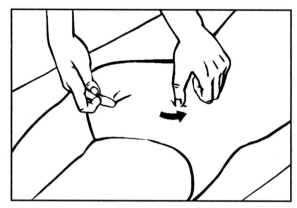

Fig.87

9 Move your fire finger to the centre of the coccyx and do gentle rotating stimulation. Repeat step 8.

10 Now contact the side of the coccyx nearest you with a gentle rotating stimulation with your right fire finger. Repeat step 8 but stimulating her left buttock with your left thumb. Keep rotating contact areas on the coccyx until the soreness is gone or you feel energy flowing.

COLON TREATMENT

The purpose of this treatment is to stimulate energy in the colon. This treatment is useful for constipation, colitis, spastic colon, gas, etc.

This is a reflex treatment for the colon. The reflexes that lie between the tibia and fibula are air element reflexes and relate both to the quality of movement in the bowels and the gases contained in the colon. These reflexes are created by the imprinting of cosmic energy waves flowing through the body whilst the embryo is in the womb.

The first part of the manipulation is a stimulation of the air element by working the shoulder reflexes on the ball of the foot. The second part of the manipulation combines the stimulation of the air element with direct stimulation over the colon reflexes along the calf. The physical direction of the contacts follows the anatomical direction of movement of matter in the colon, but is against the energetic flow in the calves and so the manipulation is stimulating in its effect.

Long standing chronic conditions of the colon generally show up as painful points along the tibia contacts. In acute conditions of the colon, such as those induced when travelling when the colon has to cope with lack of physical movement and changes in diet, relief can be obtained by working the colon reflexes on the arms, which lie between the radius and the ulna. Connect sore points on the arm with a flexing of the palm of the hand. As before begin on the right forearm to follow the anatomical flow of the movement of matter through the colon.

Colon treatment should be combined with any necessary dietary reform and colon cleansing practices where applicable.

Client is on her back.

Step 1 Stand alongside her right lower leg.

2 Grasp the sole of her right foot so that the tips of your fingers are just below the bottom joints of her toes (Fig. 88). The heel of your right hand is on top of the foot.

3 Extend and release client's foot several times. As you extend the foot (away from her head) your fingertips press on the bottom of her foot below the toe joints. Hold the extended position for a moment and then release. This stimulates the positive brachial plexus (respiratory centre) by reflex action for better air intake and gas release from the colon.

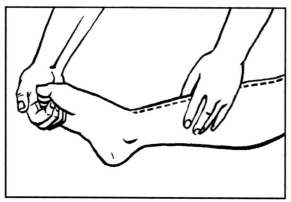

Fig.88

4 With the thumb of your left hand locate the tibia bone on the lower leg and feel for the edge of it closest to you. The space or groove between the tibia and fibula is the location of very important colon reflexes. On the right leg the reflexes are for the ascending portion of the colon and the first half of the transverse colon. The left leg contains the reflexes to the left half of the transverse colon and the descending colon (Figs. 89 and 90). The cecum is at the right ankle. As you move up the right leg, the leg areas correspond to the areas on the colon (right side). The right knee is the middle of the transverse colon. The left knee is the middle of the transverse colon on the left side. The left leg as you move down follows the path of the colon. The left ankle represents the sigmoid portion of the colon (Figs. 89 and 90). Try to visualise the tibia reflexes and how they follow the path of the colon.

127

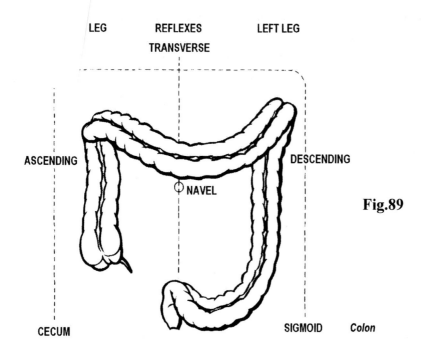

LEG   REFLEXES   LEFT LEG

TRANSVERSE

ASCENDING

DESCENDING

NAVEL

Fig.89

CECUM

SIGMOID   *Colon*

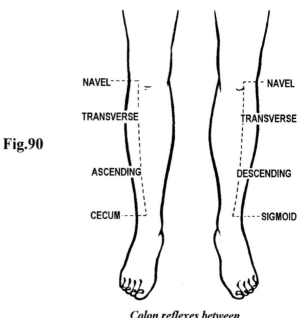

Fig.90

NAVEL

TRANSVERSE

ASCENDING

CECUM

NAVEL

TRANSVERSE

DESCENDING

SIGMOID

Colon reflexes between
tibia and fibula bones

128

Step 5 Starting at the right ankle (cecum), alternately extend the foot and then press in the groove between the tibia and fibula bones with your left thumb. Move up the right leg inch by inch. Look for sore or tender spots. For each tender spot alternately stimulate it with the foot extension for 1 minute. If the leg area is still tender, then go to step 6. If it is not, continue along the lower leg reflexes.

6 For persistently tender leg reflexes, move your right thumb to the tender spot. With your left hand (fingertips) find the spot on the colon to which it reflexes. It will usually be tender to the touch (Fig. 91). Very gently alternate stimulation on the colon itself and the leg. Tracing the reflexes to the body itself is a major part of the art and science of Polarity Therapy. Be relaxed. Remember that the tender spots reveal blocked energy. When the tenderness disappears, the energy has been released and this is the purpose of the manipulations. When you have reached the right knee you are reflexing to the middle of the transverse colon in the area of the navel.

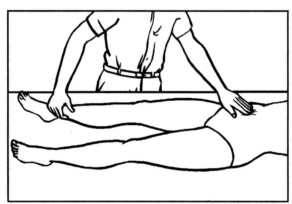

Fig.91

7 Repeat steps 1 - 6 on client's left side. Start at the left knee and work down towards her left ankle (sigmoid area).

8 To complete the colon treatment stand on client's right side. Place your left hand on the back of her neck in the area of the cervical vertebrae. Place your right hand over the colon area where it begins to transverse. This is called the hepatic flexure. Hep means liver so the colon turns (flexes) at the area of the liver which is on the right side of the body (Fig. 92).

129

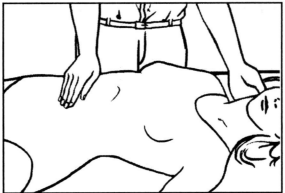

Fig 92

Step 9 Hold for 2 minutes without stimulation. Feel for energy.

10 Repeat steps 8-9 on client's left side. Your right hand is on the cervical vertebrae and your left on the splenic flexure. This is the part of the colon where it begins to descend in the area of the spleen.

Note: Steps 8 and 9 balance the neck (positive) pole with the colon (negative) pole. The neuter pole is the knees. This triune relationship is that of the astrological earth signs and the parts of the body that they rule (Taurus - the neck, Capricorn - the knees, and Virgo - the bowels).

KNEE PAIN TREATMENT

This technique uses the pinpoint energy release concept used in the pelvic release and releasing neck tension. It uses the air and fire fingers to release energy blocks around the knee and activates the deep currents of energy that cross over in the joint by making diagonal contacts through the centre.

When a blockage will not release then changing the fingers often helps; i.e. putting the fire finger where the air finger was and vice versa. This means of working can be adopted for any joint in the body.

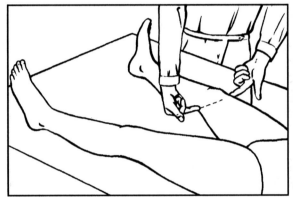

Fig.93

Step 1   Sit or stand alongside client's knee.
     2   With the air finger of either hand look for sore spots on top of the knee around the knee cap, around the inside of the knee and the outside of the knee. (Fig. 93).
     3   For each sore spot you find with your air finger, draw an imaginary line through the centre of the knee to a point diagonally opposite it. Find a sore spot with the fire finger of the other hand in this area (Fig. 93).
     4   Alternately stimulate each spot gently until soreness disappears. Hold and feel after stimulating each spot.

Note: Afterwards it is important to connect the knee to its positive and neuter poles in the neck and colon. You can also balance the knee with the joints above and below (hip/ankle).

HIP TREATMENT

This is a treatment for the relief of spasms and pain in the muscles of the hip. It is a balancing by contour which states that parts of the body that look alike or are constructed alike have a strong energetic relationship. It releases the hips by polarising them with the positive pole at the shoulders. It has a releasing effect on the diaphragm as it lies midway between the shoulders (+) and the pelvis (-). The push/pull action employed also helps to free up the spinal vertebrae and you will sometimes hear them re-adjust with a click as you are working, although this is not the purpose of the technique. The hip joint also reflexes to the ear and the jaw joint so problems in these areas can be resolved by working out tension in the hips and then polarising the two.

Remember that all the major joints in the body have a definite reflex or polarity relationship to each other. Many hip problems are structural in origin or as a result of problems in the digestive system and so further work in these areas may be necessary. Blocked emotional fire energy often manifests in the hips and so releasing the thighs as well can be beneficial. Astrological fire triad eyes (+), solar plexus (neutral) and thighs (-).

> *Client is on her side opposite the painful hip. Her top leg is bent so the knee is off the table (to relieve the weight of the leg).*

Step 1   Stand behind client.

    2   Fit your top hand in front of her shoulder.

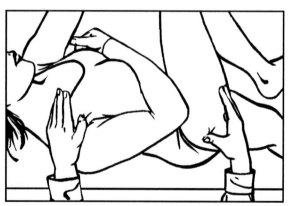

Fig.94

Step 3 The thumb of the lower hand locates sore spots in the muscles of the hip on the side nearest you (Fig. 94).

4 Pull the shoulder back towards you and rock and stimulate each of the sore spots with your thumb until soreness is gone. Stop and check periodically with client. Hold and feel for energy. Be gentle.

5 Move to the front of the client (Fig. 95).

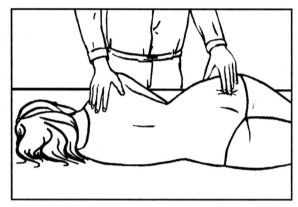

Fig.95

6 Extend her top leg so it is straight.

7 Place your upper hand on her back over the shoulder blade.

8 With the thumb of your lower hand locate tense or sore spots on the front side of the hip.

9 For each sore spot, treat as follows: pull shoulder towards you and then stimulate each sore spot gently with a rocking movement away from you until the soreness is gone. Then hold and feel for energy.

BACK PAIN TREATMENT

This treatment is a way to release blocked energy in the back muscles which manifests as pain or soreness.

The first of these manipulations connects spinal reflexes on the feet to the back. Painful areas on the back can be successfully treated using corresponding foot reflexes on the top of the feet. This vital balancing combines a negative pole contact (the foot) with a positive pole contact (the body). The second connects hand reflexes to the back. The third manipulation again releases blocked areas by pinpoint release, using positive and negative contacts. Often to effectively release back pain you should consider the use of perineal and coccyx work to release and balance the nervous system.

MANIPULATION 1

Client is on her front.

Step 1 Bend the leg which contains the reflex you are treating. Find the sore spot on top of the foot with your thumb (Fig. 96).

Fig.96

2 Place the fingers of the other bland on the sore area of the back which corresponds to the foot area (see Foot Reflex Treatment, p. 97).

Step 3 Alternately stimulate both areas until they are no longer sore. Stop periodically and check with your client.

MANIPULATION 2

Client is on her back.

Step 1 Contact the reflexes on the back of the hand and the top of the feet which correspond to the painful area of her back (see Foot and Hand Reflex Treatment, p. 145).

   2 Alternately stimulate these spots with your thumbs for several minutes, until energy flows or soreness lessens.

MANIPULATION 3 (similar to the pelvic release)

Client is on her back.

Step 1 Stand at the side you are treating.

   2 With the air finger of either hand locate a sore spot on her back.

   3 For each tender spot find a corresponding tender spot on the front of her body with the fire finger of your other hand (Fig. 97). This spot is opposite the sore spot on the back.

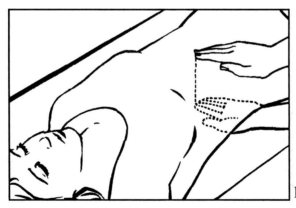

Fig.97

   4 Alternately stimulate both spots until the soreness disappears. Hold and feel the energy flow.

   5 Repeat steps 2 - 4 on each tender spot in the area of her back that hurts.

VERTEBRAE PAIN TREATMENT

A treatment to unblock energy in the vertebrae of the spine.

This treatment uses diagonal contacts between the ether and air fingers of each hand. Every vertebra is a polarised crossover point of energy waves. The right side is positive and the left side is negative, and the crossover is bi-polar from the positive right side above to the negative left articulation below it. The vertebrae above and below a sore vertebrae are treated because it is these which are fixed in their range of movement and which throw an excessive load on the vertebra in between.

Client is on her front

Step 1   Locate sore vertebra by pressing on the spinous process with your air finger. Soreness indicates blocked energy in the spinal membranes. It is caused by an energy block in the vertebrae above and below it. Make a contact on the sides of the vertebrae above and below the sore one with your air finger and thumb of each hand (Fig. 98). Alternately stimulate these points for 1 minute. Continue until the soreness of the middle vertebra is gone or lessened.

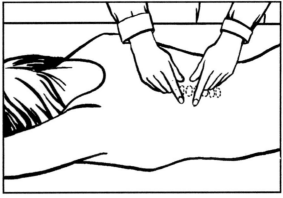

Fig.98

Step 2 Now release the air finger from the lower vertebra and the thumb from the upper vertebra. You have now created a diagonal contact through the sore vertebra (Fig. 99). Alternate stimulation until you feel energy (30 seconds to 1 minute).

3 Now create another diagonal contact with your thumb on the upper vertebra and the air finger on the lower vertebra. Alternately stimulate these points as in step 2. Check the spinous process of the vertebra in the middle. If it is still sore repeat steps 1, 2 and 3.

Fig.99

This treatment may also be done with the client seated. The same is true of the following two spinal treatments. Severe spinal pain may mean it is more comfortable for the client to be seated.

SPINAL TREATMENT

In this treatment the aim is to balance the life energy flowing through the spinal nerves to the organs, tissues, and cells of the body.

This treatment stimulates the sympathetic nerve ganglia that lie along either side of the spine. It also activates the ether current line. It influences the energy currents as they crossover at each vertebra. The technique is a balancing of the atlas as the positive pole of all the spinal vertebrae with each individual vertebra below it. The treatment begins from the most negative vertebra (5th lumbar) and works upwards.

When deciding on the contact area for each individual vertebrae remember that they vary in size enormously from being very large in the lumbar region to very small in the neck. Adjust your contact positions accordingly. It is also possible to stimulate the parasympathetic reflexes to the spinal vertebrae by contacting either side of the spine on the air current line where the parasympathetic reflexes lie by simply increasing the lateral space between your thumb and air finger.

> *Client is on her front, her head in a face cradle or split cushion so the spine is straight.*

Step 1 Stand on her left side.

 2 Place your left thumb and air finger on either side of her spine just below the occipital ridge, at the atlas or first cervical vertebra (Fig. 100).

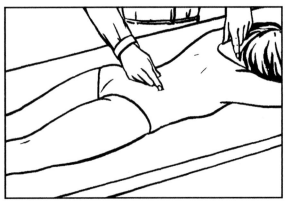

Fig.100

Step 3 Place your right thumb and air finger on either side of the fifth lumbar vertebra. This is the last lumbar vertebra found just above the sacral base.

4 While holding the neck contact with the left hand, gently stimulate the lumbar vertebra for 15 - 30 seconds with a back and forth or up and down movement. Stop and feel for the flow of energy. Repeat if necessary.

5 Repeat step 3 on each vertebra in succession, until you reach the second cervical vertebra. The upper hand remains in place.

LATERAL SPINAL BALANCING

This treatment balances the nerves on either side of spine. This simple technique balances the vertebrae laterally and has an impact on the sympathetic nerve ganglia at each vertebral level that is being treated. Vibratory impulses can be used in specific directions to help to reposition vertebrae that have rotated in their articulation. It can also be used to release gas that has collected near the spine though in this case it works best with the client sitting upright (see Gas-Releasing Treatment, p. 64).

Client is on her front.

Step 1 Beginning with the cervical vertebrae in the neck, use a double thumb contact along each side of the spine. Alternately stimulate along each side of the vertebrae in a gentle rocking motion. Hold and feel for energy or until soreness disappears (Fig.101).

2 Continue to balance all the other vertebrae or sore areas.

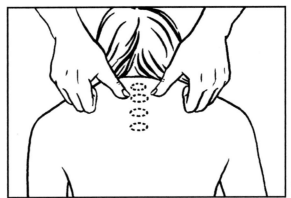

Fig.101

SHORT LEG TREATMENT

This is a structural technique that repositions the sacrum to release the short leg. The first manipulation is a very gentle non-specific release of the energy in the sacrum by polarising the three corners. The second manipulation is a passive mobilisation of the hip joint coupled with firm steady pressure over tight muscles in the buttocks that may be pulling the sacrum into imbalance (e.g. the piriformis muscle).

MANIPULATION 1

Client is on her back.

Step 1 Stand at her feet. Check to see which leg is shorter. To do this, grasp both heels and gently pull the legs toward you so they are taut. Look at the levels of the prominent bones on the inside of the ankles. The bone furthest from you is the short leg. You can also determine the short leg by looking at her heels.

   2 Have client turn over onto her abdomen.

   3 Stand at her short-leg side.

   4 Locate the sacrum of the spine. It is an inverted triangle with its apex above the coccyx and is based below the 5th or last lumbar vertebra. It is right above the crack in the buttocks in the lower back.

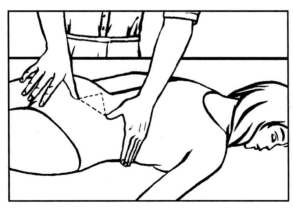

Fig.102

Step 5 Place one thumb on the apex and your, other thumb on the corner of the sacral base closest to your side.

6 Alternate stimulation for 1 - 2 minutes. Feel the energy.

7 Move your top thumb to the other corner of the sacral base and alternate stimulation for 1 - 2 minutes (Fig. 102).

MANIPULATION 2

Client is on her front.

Step 1 With the thumb locate a sore spot in the hip of her short leg around the head of the femur bone (hip joint). Hold this spot firmly with your thumb.

2 With your other hand grasp her ankle and lift the leg to a right angle (Fig. 103).

3 Rotate the entire leg towards you 20 times. Then lower her leg.

4 Have client turn over and re-check the leg lengths. Repeat if necessary.

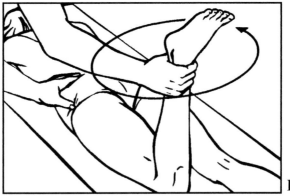

Fig.103

SCIATICA TREATMENT

This session can be helpful in cases of inflammation of the sciatic nerve.

This technique uses foot flexion to stretch the muscles along the back of the leg and buttock and their various attachments to the hips and pelvis. The movement has a releasing and decompressing effect on the sacrum, its articulation and the fifth lumbar vertebrae. This technique can be accomplished more easily on the floor where you can kneel and support the client's leg against you, especially useful for clients that have long and heavy legs. Where there is excessive pain and the client is unable to lift the leg, try working the perineal floor on the sorest side and taking the energy down the leg to the ankle before attempting this manipulation.

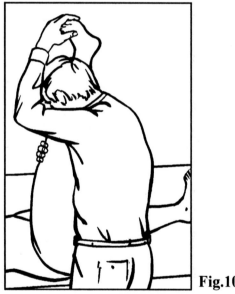

Fig.104

Client is on her back.

Step 1 Stand on client's right side.

    2 Face the table with your feet towards it. Rotate your left leg 90° to the left.

3 Then place her right leg on your right shoulder. Your right leg should be against the table.
4 Your right hand is placed above her knee to keep her leg straight. With your left hand hold her toes. (Fig. 104)
5 Have client inhale and exhale. On the exhale gently flex the toes. On the inhale, relax the flexion.
6 Repeat several times increasing the flexion each time.
7 Then bend her leg and hold her knee with your left hand and her ankle with your right, for one minute. Feel for energy.
Repeat on opposite side when needed reversing hand and foot contacts above as shown.

USING FOOT AND HAND REFLEXES TO STIMULATE AND BALANCE THE LIFE ENERGY

A reflex is any point along an energy current which, when stimulated, sends energy to other places along the same current. Foot reflexology as usually practiced is limited to the foot pole only. In Polarity Therapy, the foot contacts are combined with the hand reflexes and the body very effectively to unblock the life energy. For those of you who know foot reflexology, try combining the contacts as described below and see if your treatments are enhanced.

When the hand reflexes are sorest then you are dealing with an acute condition, if the feet are more sore than the hands it is a chronic condition.

If you memorise the position of the navel and the shoulders according to the chart, finding other parts will be easy. We are treating energy in specific zones of the body rather than specific organs.

Figures 105 and 106 show different ways of locating foot and hand reflexes which relate to body areas and vice versa.

Figure 105 shows the soles of the feet superimposed over the front of the body. Reflexes to the body parts shown are approximately where they show on the feet.

Figure 106 shows how zone areas of the foot and hand are reflexes to the zone areas on the body.

Note: The right foot and hand contain reflexes to the right side of the body. The left foot and hand contain reflexes to the left side of the body. The way to know if you are in the correct reflex is that corresponding areas (body, foot and hand) will all be tender or sore.

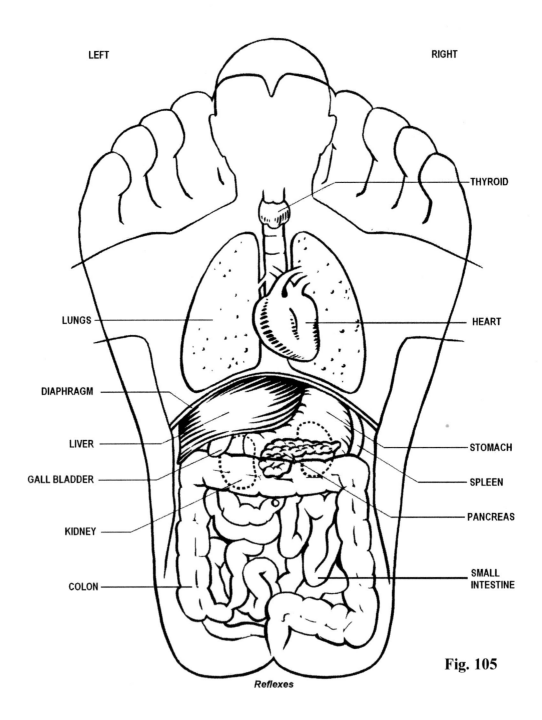

LEFT

RIGHT

THYROID

LUNGS

HEART

DIAPHRAGM

LIVER

STOMACH

GALL BLADDER

SPLEEN

PANCREAS

KIDNEY

COLON

SMALL
INTESTINE

Reflexes

Fig. 105

146

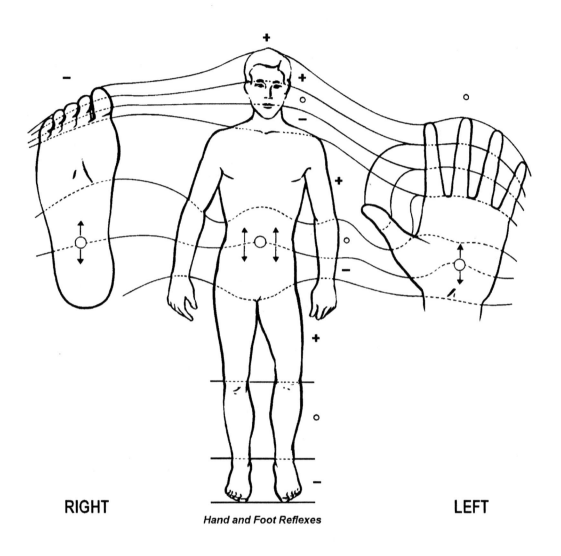

RIGHT

LEFT

Hand and Foot Reflexes

Fig.106

147

TO DETERMINE THE LOCATION OF ENERGY BLOCKS AND TO THEN STIMULATE THOSE BLOCKED AREAS.

When treating the back of the body, client lies on her abdomen. When treating the front of the body she lies on her side or on her back. Remember that the top of the foot and back of the hands reflex to the back of the body; sole of the foot and palm of the hand to the front of the body.

Step 1 Contact the foot or negative pole (-) with your thumb.
    2 With your other thumb contact the same place on the hand or neuter (0) pole.
    3 Alternately stimulate for several minutes. Feel for energy flowing.
    4 Remove the hand contact and place your fingers on the reflexed body area. Hold this while you firmly but gently stimulate the foot. If the foot reflex is more tender than the hands, it means a chronic energy block. If the hand is more sore it means an acute energy block.
    5 Contact the body part and the related hand reflex area (Fig. 106). Alternately stimulate for several minutes.

THE FIVE POINTED STAR

The five-pointed star is one of the most useful and important treatments in Polarity Therapy.

The five-pointed star is created by geometric lines of force. It is an interference pattern of energy in the body. That is to say, it is not a primary pattern of energy having its own particular source, but it is established as a result of the interaction of all the primary flows of energy. It is an example of the hermetic principle of correspondence "as above, so below." That which is above is reflected in the area below and that which is below has a representation above which governs it. This means that many dysfunctions arising below the diaphragm are reflected upwards through the star pattern to be established as painful symptoms in the shoulders, neck and head.

The top of the star is at the throat centre which is the source of the current in the etheric field. In the pelvic basin at the bottom is the sum total force of all sensory tension and emotional frustration. The two lowest points of the star rest here (Fig. 107).

It is at these lower points that individual vital force, the electromagnetic currents and the gravity pull of the earth intersect. These centres of vital and emotional energy located in the pelvis, can be released naturally by inhibiting the attachments of the abdominal muscles to the pelvic bones, the psoas and iliacus muscles. Releasing these pelvic muscles causes a release to the shoulders and occipital and cervical areas.

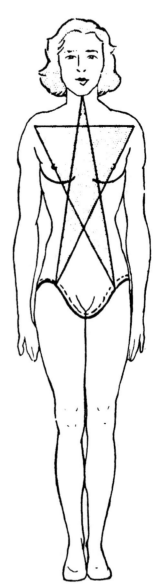

Fig.107

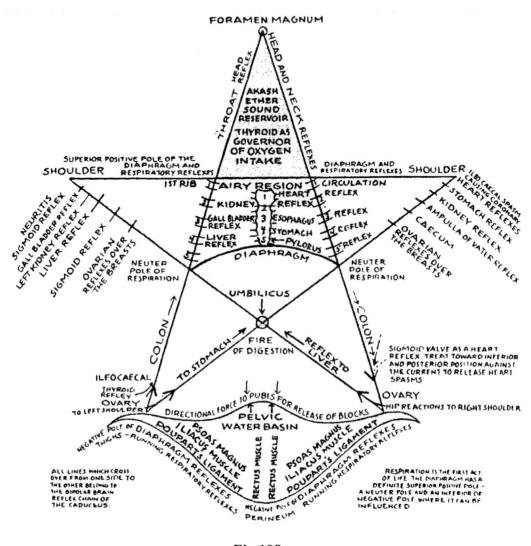

Fig.108

If you study Fig.108 it is easy to see how a complex web of reflexes is established. All the organs which the lines of force pass over in their ascending flow have their reflexes above the diaphragm in exactly the same order as the one below, e.g. the ovaries and pelvic organs have their reflexes in the breasts.

The star has its lower points in the water oval of the pelvis and its upper points in the air oval at the shoulders and the ether oval at the neck. Dr. Stone described it as a symbol of invagination - that is the movement of energy going inward and upwards, and for this reason it is considered a feminine, evolutionary pattern although both sexes possess it.

The five pointed star is a cross over pattern and so brings into play the caduceus currents, which in turn activate the chakras, and thereby influence all the elements. It can have a releasing effect on the diaphragm and mid-abdominal transition areas so it plays an important part in our postural alignment and in the art of Structural Balancing.

It can be a good release for the psoas muscle when performed with deep contacts on the front of body over the Pouparts ligament, and when performed on the back of the body releases sympathetic nerve blocks over the shoulders and buttocks. It can effectively be utilised to treat neck, shoulder, digestive, pelvic, hip, back problems and more. It can also play an active part in helping to bring emotions held below the diaphragm up to the surface to be expressed through the throat. Superimposed on the human body it has become the symbol of man.

Tension in the front of the body is usually functional, a reflex from the visceral organs. Soreness and tension over any organ is nature's way of letting us know that those organs are blocked. Releasing the energy blocks (Fig. 108) is done by directional contacts on the line of force.

The arrows on or alongside the lines indicate the directional pressure used in the manipulation. It is very important to line up your hands, fingers, forearms and upper arms at the proper angle and hold long enough to create a push of the molecules and atoms in the current (felt as a release). The directions used are either towards the head and neck on the same side or towards the opposite shoulder.

Client is on her back.

Step 1 Place both hands with the fingertips arranged so they are level, on the inside of the top of the pelvic bone (over the Poupart's ligament) on the left side.

   2 Align both hands, wrists and forearms in the direction of either the throat or the right shoulder (shown by arrow), depending on which direction of energy flow you wish to stimulate (Fig. 109).

   3 Push gently downwards into the abdomen and then up towards the shoulder or throat. It is a gentle, scooping movement of about 2 inches. Move the hands back to the pelvic bone and repeat until you feel a definite release of the muscles. Be *very gentle* as this area is often very tender. Work to release the muscles and relieve any soreness. If the muscles are very tight, firm steady pressure applied to the muscles (the hands formed into fists and using the flat of the fist to apply the pressure) may help the muscles to relax. Keep the hands and arms aligned as in step 2. Once the muscles have begun to relax proceed using the fingertips as described.

   4 Work any of the lines of force as required and repeat on the other side if necessary.

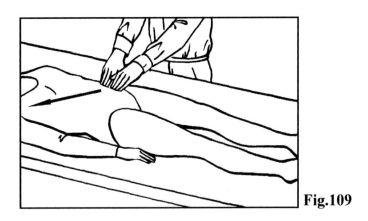

Fig.109

6 POLARITY YOGA

Do you get enough exercise? Most of us don't. Yet exercise is one of the most important requirements for health and vitality.

Exercise can too easily become a dull routine, often done grudgingly. It's therefore important that our approach to exercise is one of concentration and joy, as we realise we are stimulating the body's life energy and rejuvenating every cell.

The following Polarity Yoga exercises are a series of easy stretching postures based on the principle of stimulating and releasing the flow of energy. In his book "Health Building," Dr Stone recommends regular practice of these exercises several times a day for only a few minutes at a time.

The essential difference between Polarity Yoga and static stretching postures lies in the fact that, in Polarity exercises, once the appropriate position is assumed you use gentle rhythmic movements in various directions. This creates a gentle dynamo like charge through the body's energy fields as the body's energy interacts with the earth's own energy field. We all know how calming it is to sit in a rocking chair and how rocking the body backwards and forwards can make pain more bearable; this is because the body is being given a gentle Polarity treatment.

Polarity Yoga Exercises

These postures should be done in the centre of a room away from any furniture. It's ideal to wear loose clothing and work on a soft mat or rug. Feet should be flat on the floor. Shoes may be worn, or something to elevate the heels, e.g. a book. After becoming more practiced in these postures, bare feet without any heel support is preferable.

The Squat

The squat postures release and balance the vital energy blocked in the pelvis. This will aid in the elimination of wastes and gases, and promote a better intake of oxygen and air. These postures also help produce mental calmness and peace.

Place feet 6 inches apart at the heels and 12 inches at the toes. This will vary from person to person depending on flexibility. Gently rock up and down a little at a time until the posture in Fig. 110 is attained or you are as far down as you can comfortably be.

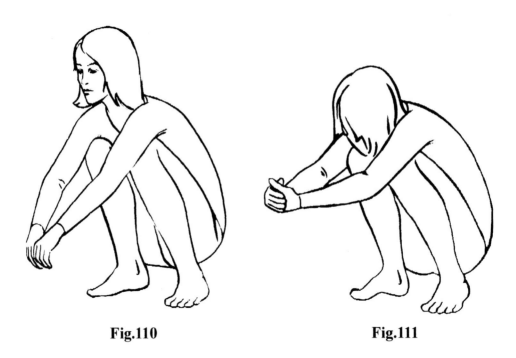

Fig.110   **Fig.111**

FIG. 110 In this position start rocking front to back, then side to side. Rotate the pelvis in both directions. Hands are stretched out over the knees Do this for 1-2 minutes.
FIG. 111 Without using any force wrap your arms around the outside of the knees which are pushed together. Inhale deeply to push and stretch from the inside of the body out. Release the breath with a grunt. The head is bent forward to stretch the spine and promote relaxation.

This posture is excellent for releasing gases, constipation, sagging abdomen and freeing the hip joints. While in this position, rock from side to side, forward and back, then rotate your pelvis. 1-2 minutes will activate the life-energy currents.

Youth Posture

Begin the same as in fig. 110. For more stretch have the feet further apart (heels 12 inches and toes 24 inches). Distance will vary according to flexibility. Don't exert any force. Remember, it is not the accomplishment of the posture but the stimulation of the energy currents that is important. Be comfortable. Place arms inside the knees and push outward. Thumbs are placed next to the nose and eyebrow on each side. The head rests on the thumbs for relaxation of the neck (Fig. 112). Then rock as in the other postures. This activates a different set of muscles to those worked in the narrow squat and releases stagnant energy. Squat exercises are good for strengthening the back and spine, when you are fatigued, have trouble sleeping or are emotionally upset. Practice these for 3- 5 minutes each day and you will see the results.

Fig.112

Sinus Clearing Exercise (Scissor Kick)

Lie face down on the floor, resting your head on your hands. Separate your legs so that they form a 'V' shape far enough apart so that you can feel a good stretch in the hip joints. Flex the legs so they are at right angles to the floor (Fig. 113). Now cross and uncross your legs in a scissor-like motion for about 5-10 minutes. Make sure your legs pass each other as you cross them (Fig. 114). This exercise may be repeated as often as necessary until you feel the head clear and the sinuses and nostrils open. The dynamic effect in this exercise is created by the stimulation of the pubic bone which reflexes to the sphenoid bone which is located in the area of the sinuses.

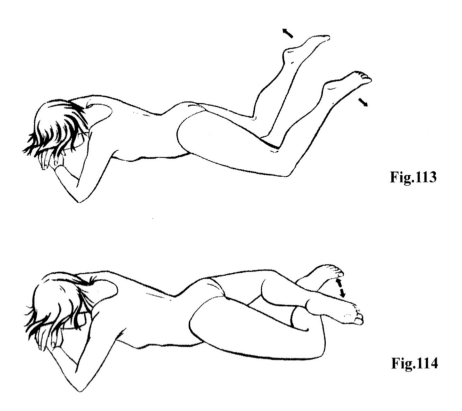

Fig.113

Fig.114

The Cliffhanger

This exercise works on the chest, shoulders, and the brachial plexus, affecting the air and fire elements in the body, aiding respiration and digestion.

Take a position with your feet shoulder width apart, about 18 inches in front of a table or ledge about waist high, for use as a support. Put your hands behind you palm down on the supporting surface with the fingers pointing forwards (Fig. 115). Breathe in deeply and sink your body downwards towards the floor without leaning forwards so that your spine stays close to the edge of the table but not touching it (Fig. 116). Go down as far as you can, keeping the body relaxed. Stay down and, breathing deeply, allow your body to sink a little lower on each exhalation. This exercise may also be done using a loud HAAA! sound on each exhalation to release energy.

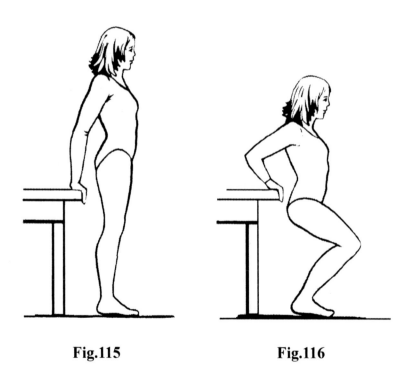

Fig.115   **Fig.116**

Spinal Rolling

This exercise helps loosen up all the joints and also massages the spine. It is a good preliminary exercise to use before any other Polarity Yoga exercises.

Sit on the floor on a carpet or mat with your knees bent. Place your hands behind your thighs just above the knees. Then tuck your chin gently toward your chest and keep it there (Fig. 117). Slowly roll backwards as you pull your knees towards you; when you stop rolling backwards, push your feet towards the floor and roll forwards this should be a relaxed, continuous movement. Roll back and forth for 2 minutes or more while breathing deeply.

Fig.117

Cat Walk

This exercise, walking like a cat, helps to coordinate both sides of the brain. It also stimulates the pelvis and abdomen.

If you observe or visualise a cat walking you'll notice that they move as follows: First, the right front paw moves forward; then the left rear paw moves forward. Next, the left front paw moves forward; then the right rear paw moves forward.

Practice this walk while exaggerating the movements. Begin by leaning forward from a standing position with your arms held straight until they touch the floor, keeping the legs as straight as possible (Fig. 118). Now move the right hand forward about 6-8 inches, followed by the left foot about the same distance. Then move the left hand, followed by the right foot; then the right hand again and so on. The distance you move the arms and feet depends upon your flexibility. Move backwards and forwards across a large area 4-6 times daily.

Fig.118

Working Calf-and-Foot Reflexes (Calf Cruncher)

This exercise combines movement with stimulation of the reflexes in the Achilles tendon (lower back), the calves of the legs (colon) and the soles of the feet (the entire body).

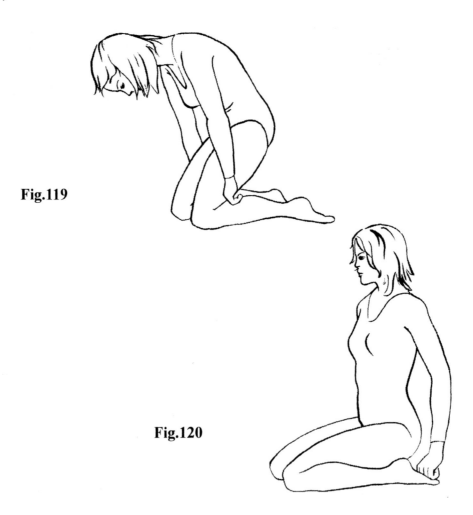

Fig.119

Fig.120

Begin by kneeling on the floor with your toes extended behind you. Place your fists behind you so that your knuckles (second joint) are contacting the area just below your knees on your calves (Fig. 119). Now gently rock backwards and forwards.

As you rock backwards press down on your calves with your knuckles, and then release the pressure as you lean forwards. Repeat the rocking backwards and forwards, moving your knuckles inch by inch down your calves towards the heels. When you find tender or sensitive places stay on that spot, repeat the pressure then rock backwards and forwards for a while until the tenderness disappears. Breathe into the sensitive spot, exhaling as you press; making a sound as you exhale (Aaah!) helps to move energy. Keep your mouth open and jaw relaxed throughout this exercise. Stop when you reach the point where the Achilles tendon meets the heel. After finishing, grasp your right heel with your right hand and place your left hand on your front fontanel. Rock backwards and forwards in this position for 1 minute. Then change hands (left on left heel right on front fontanel) and repeat.

Now, in the same position, work down the soles of your feet pressing and releasing with your knuckles, staying on any sensitive areas to release the tenderness (Fig. 120). Continue down to the toe joints but be very gentle as the toe joints can be very sensitive. Keep your breathing deep and even. Relax the body as much as possible. This exercise should be done 1-2 times daily.

Breathing

Most people breathe incorrectly, especially older people. Correct breathing is done abdominally. To Practice this, do the following:

Lie on your back and place your hands on your abdomen. Slowly inhale and, while doing this, imagine that you are inflating a balloon which is in your abdomen under your hands. After a complete inhalation, slowly exhale and imagine that the balloon is deflating. Repeat this ten times morning and evening.

It is very useful to Practice this breathing exercise out of doors or in front of an open window while standing. Correct breathing aids digestion as the air fans the fire of digestion.

Self-Healing Visualisation

It is possible by using our minds to direct life energy to any part of the body that needs healing.

This is done by gently tensing, then relaxing that part of the body. Tense again and mentally count from 1 to 10 while visualising the disease in that part of the body being electrocuted with powerful healing energy. You may systematically tense and relax all your muscle groups, concentrating on the muscles being tensed. Hold tension for up to 15 seconds but not to the point of discomfort.

You may aid your concentration by visualising light bombarding the muscle being tensed. To work on your muscle groups begin with the left foot, curling the toes against the sole of the foot. Hold for up to 15 seconds, then relax. Repeat with the right foot. Relax. Follow this procedure for the entire body in the following order:

left foot then right foot
left calf then right calf
left thigh then right thigh
left buttock then right buttock
abdomen below the navel
abdomen above the navel
left hand then right hand
left forearm then right forearm
left bicep then right bicep
left side of chest then right side of chest
left side of neck then right side of neck.

This procedure will promote relaxation and healing and can be done by anyone.
These tension-relaxation exercises done two times daily are very beneficial to your overall health, e.g. they can help reduce high blood pressure. Any time you need to relax, tense the entire body gently, then relax. Remain still, experiencing and enjoying the calmness of your body.

For the very ill, these exercises can just be done mentally in the imagination and be just as beneficial.

Fresh Air and Exercise

Deep breathing exercises done out of doors ensure that all body cells are bathed in oxygen necessary for their optimum functioning. Try the following exercise done while walking outside:

First, exhale quickly through the mouth and nostrils. Then inhale slowly through the nostrils counting mentally from 1 to 12. Hold the breath, counting to 6. Exhale through the mouth and nostrils, counting to 6. Counts are approximately 2 per second.

Repeat this 24 times when out walking.

Air causes movement of energy in the body. Deep breathing helps the lungs and circulation to function more effectively so that all cells receive this vital life energy.

Sun Light and Life Energy

Without the nourishing rays of the sun, there would be no life. The sun's ultra-violet rays contain a magical healing power that is kept active by our body's life energy. It is this life energy that vitalises and chemicalises the sun's energy. Heliotropic methods of healing are those which combine sunlight and life energy. An effective way of achieving this healing is to gently and rapidly rub the part of the body that you wish to heal while exposing it to the sun. At the same time, imagine that the life energy of the sun is mixing with the energy in your fingers to saturate the body part being rubbed with a healing light.

A short sunbath of 10 minutes daily to both sides of the body (preferably at noon), and for three hours (in the summer this should be done in short periods adding up to three hours in total so as to avoid sunburn) at the weekend will saturate the body with a healing current that will last for three months. This life energy supplied to the body helps destroy harmful microbes.

7 DIET AND NUTRITION

The unimpeded and plentiful flow of life energy in the human body is the most important factor in maintaining health and well being. The relationship between the food we eat and life energy lies in the fact that it is through diet that the body acquires a large proportion of the energy required to replenish its energy fields. The attraction of polarity energy fields is the essence of a good diet. Food and drink must be first broken down by the body's energies and the energy particles released so that they can be absorbed as building blocks and fitted into the normal function of the body.

As described earlier (p. 19 - 22) matter and energy are classified into five elements; ether, air, fire, water and earth. The food we eat can be classified according to its elemental nature. As the energy fields become depleted they are recharged by the energetic essence of food. We need to replace the solids (earth), liquids (water), gases (air) and heat (fire) used by the body on a daily basis by eating a variety of foods representing these four elements.

This classification of food goes beyond the standard categories of proteins, carbohydrates, vitamins, minerals, etc., as being the only necessities of good nutrition. The mere chemical approach is not always the answer, the body's energy requirements must also be taken into account. The strong craving for certain foods can be explained as the body's attempt to attract and replenish its depleted energies through the elements contained in those foods. The following groups show the four elements and the foods which help sustain them.

Ether
The ether element in the body is affected by the appearance, aroma, and the way in which the food we eat is served.

Air
This element is associated with action in the body and is especially needed by highly nervous and active people. Foods in this category are yeasts and their products, fruits (especially citrus), nuts, fermented cheeses and other dairy products such as yogurt, keifer, acidophilus and buttermilk.

Fire
Foods in this category replace expended energy and warmth and are best suited for persons with great mental and physical drive. Foods in this category include seeds, such as sesame and sunflower, papaya, most grains (wheat, spelt, rye etc) and legumes (beans) which are rich in starch and protein.

Water
These foods include green leafy vegetables, cucumbers, celery, squash, pumpkin, melons, milk and sea foods (kelp, dulse, etc.). Highly emotional people need watery foods.

Earth
These are needed by persons with a rugged constitution who perform hard physical labour. Foods in this category include fats, starches and sugars, and tubers or root vegetables which grow under the ground such as potatoes, turnips, carrots, beets, onions and garlic. These satisfy hunger and are rich in minerals.

Remember: each individual should select the foods that he can best digest and utilise.

Even taking the elemental needs of the body into account it is not so much what we eat but what we can digest that determines our state of health. Energy blocks can obstruct the digestion and assimilation of food and the absorption of their energy essence even if that particular energy essence is sorely needed to revitalise the body. Just as importantly, the better the quality of the food the more likely we will be able to digest it.

Natural, whole and pure foods contribute to good health by calming the mind, thus permitting the life energy to flow uninterrupted. Raw fruits, vegetables and nuts, for those who can assimilate them, have a strengthening effect on the mind and body. Foods such as meat, which retains the vibrations of fear, pain and anger of the dying animal, are disturbing to the mind, robbing it of its power to awaken and direct life energy to heal the body. The same is true of denatured foods, those which contain artificial preservatives, additives, colouring, etc. and food which has had its natural properties destroyed through improper cooking and preparation.

Polarity Purifying Diet

If you have any health problems, e.g. constipation, poor digestion, high blood pressure, arthritis, rheumatism, pain, swelling, congestion, toxicity and overweight, first and foremost the body needs to be restored to normal functioning. This is best done through the aid of a purifying diet. The following diet was designed by Dr Stone.

MORNING
This is the best time for flushing out the system and cleansing it. Only liquids are taken. Start with a drink to flush out the liver. This is made with:

Juice of several oranges or a grapefruit
Juice of 1/2 lemon or lime (4-6 tablespoons)
2-3   tablespoons of cold-pressed olive oil or sesame oil
1-3   cloves of crushed garlic

Blend and drink.

The 'liver flush' is followed by a herbal tea made by boiling three cups of water and adding several thin slices of fresh ginger root. This mixture is poured over one teaspoon each of licorice root, fennel seed, fenugreek seed and peppermint leaves. Prepare the tea first and let it steep while you make the 'liver flush' drink. Two hours later have 8 ounces or more of fresh vegetable juice made from carrots, beets, celery and any greens. Sip slowly, salivating each mouthful thoroughly.

LUNCH
Raw salad which includes sprouts (alfalfa, soy, fenugreek, mung, etc.), grated vegetables and fresh greens. A dressing of cold pressed almond, olive or sesame oil with lemon juice, ginger and garlic is beneficial as well as tasty. Fruit can be used for dessert (apples, pears, grapes, mango, papaya, dates, raisins, etc.). If still hungry, a dish of plain baked or steamed vegetables with cooked or sprouted beans is filling and good for you. The pulp and residue from the vegetable juices can be boiled in water for half an hour and strained and drunk as a hot beverage. Season with onion and ginger if desired. Drink this between meals. During the afternoon have another glass of fresh raw vegetable juice. Again, use the pulp to make a hot soup and have it later in the afternoon or before bed. Chew all foods thoroughly.

DINNER

Fresh fruit plus the herbal tea. If you are very hungry, repeat the lunch meal. Fruit juices may be drunk between meals. During the purifying diet, have no milk, meat, butter, coffee or black tea. No potatoes, rice, bread, or any cereals or grains. No sugar and no fried foods. Do not use aluminium cookware.

Eating any of the above foods will nullify the excellent effects of this diet. (Note: This diet contains all the necessary protein, vitamins and minerals you need to restore health and replenish the body's energies, and can be done indefinitely without danger.) While on the diet, it is recommended that you have a hot bath daily followed by a cold shower. Flushing out the colon with a cold-water enema is also beneficial. Do not retain the water. Warm water may be used in cold climates.

Sprouts abundantly provide all the necessary elements found in nature. These are lacking and needed when we are sick. Be sure to include a variety of them daily and chew them well. Wheatgrass can be grown and added to salads or juiced. This is the most healthful green available. Learn to sprout seeds and beans and grow wheatgrass. Once you have regained health and are feeling fit, the following regimen for eating will ensure that you obtain all the necessary elements your body needs. It is a combination cleansing and building regimen.

Have one good protein, one good starch, six vegetables and two fruits daily.

BREAKFAST Fruit, cereal and one protein if desired.
LUNCH One starch, plus a salad or steamed vegetable.
DINNER 2-3 vegetables or salad, plus a protein.

You may switch lunch and dinner for convenience.

Best starches are rye, brown rice, millet and yellow cornmeal, ripe bananas, barley and squash.

Best proteins are eggs, raw milk, cheese, nuts, seeds (and their butters), soy, lentil and all beans, lean meat, fish or chicken. Avoid fat beef and pork and limit meat to three to four times a week.

60% of the diet should be raw or steamed foods.

Avoid all fried foods.

Substitute honey or pure maple syrup for sugar.

Never eat if angry or upset. This inhibits digestion. Make meal times the happiest, most relaxed time of the day.

Don't overeat.

Avoid refined, processed, canned or frozen foods.

Vary proteins, starches, vegetables, fruits and sugars from meal to meal and day to day.

Natural Remedies

There is much that can be done for yourself when ill, through diet and herbal remedies. Pierre Pannetier recommended the following recipes to alleviate specific conditions and thereby aid better health.

ACID STOMACH 1 teaspoon agar-agar, chew until liquified. Use as needed.

AGE SPOTS, NEUTRALISING RADIATION and ELIMINATING TOXINS
First Day: Add 1 lb each of sea salt and baking soda to bath. Soak for half an hour. Second Day: Add 1 tablespoon Clorox per gallon of water in bath. Soak for half an hour. Alternate the above regime for 10 days.

ALLERGIES Purify the bloodstream with herbs such as dandelion root, burdock root or red clover. Make into tea and drink 3 cups daily. Go on the Polarity purifying diet as outlined earlier.

ARTHRITIS and RHEUMATISM Alternate a stream of cold/hot water on painful joint, half a minute each, 6-7 times, daily.

ASTHMA Starch and milk-free diet with two tablespoons lemon juice before each meal and before retiring.

ATHLETE'S FOOT Lemon juice alone or combined with papaya juice. Apply freely.

BLEEDING 1 teaspoon cayenne pepper in water as a drink. Sprinkle cayenne pepper on the wound.

BROKEN BONES After cast removal rub olive oil on area of break. Sprinkle on cayenne pepper. Dip fresh comfrey leaves in hot water until they are pliable. Wrap leaves around break. Place bandage around leaves to hold them in place.

BURNS and BRUISES Cut a lemon in half. Then rub the lemon on the burn or bruised area.

CANCER Purify the bloodstream with herbs such as dandelion root, plantain, burdock root or red clover. Use chapparal (dwarf evergreen oak) foot bath each morning for 20 minutes. Make a tea and soak feet in the water (hot or warm).

CATARACTS Several drops of equal amounts of lemon juice and distilled water, into the eye three times daily.

CLEANSING REGIME For three days eat only raw apples and water (lots). Follow with half a cup cold-pressed olive oil.

PREVENTIVE FOR COLDS Use the following in winter or any time as a cleanser of the system:

1-2 carrots
1 celery (leaves & stalk)
Handful of fresh parsley
1 large onion
2-3 cloves garlic (large)
Season with thyme, rosemary and sage

Chop all ingredients. Cover with water. Bring to the boiL then cook over low heat for half an hour. Strain and save the vegetables.
Add 1-2 tablespoons cold-pressed oil before serving and
1 pinch cayenne
2 tablespoons lemon juice (or to taste)
Pinch of sea salt
Take 2-3 cups twice a week in winter.
The following day, have the vegetables for lunch.

CONSTIPATION Three 'liver flush' drinks (see p. 166) daily with extra cold-pressed oil. or grind 2 tablespoons flax seed (linseed). Soak in warm water overnight. In the morning add a little warm water, place in the blender with a little honey and a ripe banana. Blend and drink.
or
Half a cup lemon juice
Half a cup cold-pressed olive oil. Mix and take four times daily until bowels move.

CORNS and CALLOUSES Chapparal foot bath (see Cancer above).

DIARRHOEA Take the pulp of one apple mixed with lemon juice and a little honey. Sprinkle powdered cinnamon on the mixture.

HEAD CONGESTION (sinus trouble, colds, hay fever, asthma) Apply compress of grated or liquified raw potato to the jugular veins to drain them.

INDIGESTION Fresh parsley tea sipped before bedtime. Add cardamom seeds and black pepper to salads. Or take half a tablespoon of yellow mustard seeds with water half an hour before meals.

INFECTIONS Soak any of the following herbs in water (1 teaspoon to 1 cup boiling water, soak 5 minutes and drink): cloves, thyme, rosemary, sage.

PAIN Dip cabbage leaves in hot water for a few seconds. Use as a poultice on painful part of the body.

SINUSES (clogged)
4 ounces fresh horseradish (grated)
1 teaspoon garlic juice
2 ounces lemon juice
1 tablespoon honey
Mix thoroughly and take one or more teaspoons four times daily.

SKIN CONDITIONS Apply liquified or grated raw cucumber compresses.

INTESTINAL and STOMACH ULCERS Drink cabbage and carrot juice combined.

INFECTED SWELLINGS, SPLINTERS Grated raw red beets used as a compress.

VARICOSE VEINS Rub garlic on vein. Use alternating hot/cold water half a minute each, six to seven times daily, then massage with olive oil (a drop).

8 COUNSELLING FOR POSITIVE THOUGHTS AND ATTITUDES

The science of Polarity Therapy is founded on spiritual principles which exist in our lives, principles which operate no matter how unaware of them we may be. One of these principles, or laws, is that each thought creates according to its own nature.

A positive state of mind is one of the first rules of good health. When you are sincerely joyful, you are less subject to disease, for happiness attracts into the body a greater supply of life energy and distributes it to every body cell.

Dr Stone taught that the initial cause of illness begins with negative thinking. Negative thoughts and attitudes impede the flow of life energy. Thus, our digestion is affected which, in turn, results in our cells not being properly nourished and wastes not being properly eliminated. The result is dis-ease, which usually strikes that part of the body which happens to be the most susceptible due to inherited weaknesses, poor diet, lack of exercise, fresh air, etc.

Most systems of healing today treat the effects of disease rather than the causes which lie in our master computer - the mind. To be completely cured we must change our thoughts, otherwise illness will return in one form or another.

Most doctors will acknowledge that the mind is a major contributory factor to disease. It therefore stands to reason that, if the mind is so powerful, we can use it to promote healing. Thoughts are vibrations of energy moving at an extremely fast rate of speed, according to Dr Stone, faster than even sound or light. To be healthy, or to promote healing, we must utilise the power of our mind. Thoughts need to be understood and correctly applied in order to be effective in healing.

As Dr Stone stated in his first book, our mind is the creator of our body and continues to affect every cell throughout our lives. Through control of our mind, it is possible to revitalise our body at will. Our thoughts set up vibrations that initiate actions which produce the results of those thoughts. We should be very careful about our thoughts and not underestimate their power.

Avoid suggesting to your mind thoughts of sickness, lack, old age, death; thoughts of worry, fear, anger or jealousy, for these thoughts create vibrations which activate universal forces resulting in the materialisation of those thoughts. As you think, so you are. Thoughts of vitality, health, love, joy, peace and happiness will activate the same forces. Why not choose health rather than sickness? Affirmations can be used to create a positive state of body and mind. Affirmations are positive statements saturated with sincerity, conviction, faith, intuition and will power. When used correctly, affirmations have the explosive vibratory effect to create what is being affirmed.

The following are some suggestions for using affirmations:

1 Choose an affirmation which suits your needs. Example: "I enjoy vibrant health," or "I am inwardly happy and calm regardless of external circumstances."
2 Select a quiet place to Practice.
3 Free your mind from worry and restlessness.
4 Mornings upon rising and evenings before retiring are especially beneficial times.
5 Sit with eyes closed and spine straight.
6 Repeat the entire affirmation, first out loud, then in a whisper, and finally mentally. Do this 10-20 times.
7 Remember that faith motivates will and will controls the life energy in the body which is the same energy that heals us. Have faith that what you affirm will manifest itself.
8 In addition to mornings and evenings, Practice any time you have a chance (on a bus, at the laundromat, etc.).
9 When you catch yourself thinking a negative thought, change it to an affirmation.

Pierre Pannetier said, *"As Polarity Therapists we are teaching people to accept everything that is coming to them with a smile. When you are unhappy see what you are not able to accept in your life. If you can then accept it, you will be happy."*

Happiness is a soul quality. In order to find the true happiness and peace that we (the mind) now fruitlessly seek in material objects and relationships, we need to develop the soul qualities of *faith, hope, charity, humility, love, service* and *understanding.*

173

These qualities are developed through right living and meditation - practices which have been handed down to us through the ages as tools for self-realisation. They form the essence of spiritual living and healing.

There are some basic concepts concerning personal freedom which must be realised by an individual before the true soul qualities can be fully expressed. We must first understand that we are responsible for our thoughts and feelings. They are ours and we have chosen them. Pierre Pannetier said that we must be accepting of our circumstances - to be unattached and non-reactive - in order to be happy. As we become more aware of our freedom we will see that we can choose attitudes which expand our energies or those which contract them. We can choose to recoil in anger (to resist what, in fact, we have created as a result of our thoughts) or to surrender that aspect of our ego selves. This should in no way suggest being passive or repressing our emotions. On the contrary, it means that, as we learn to acknowledge all the emotional aspects which come into play in our lives, as we become more aware of our thoughts, we will lose the attachment which keeps us relentlessly tossed about by the rules of these manifestations and enter a state of deeper love and acceptance.

Apart from using the power of affirmation we can change our thoughts through the releasing of deep-seated stimuli-response emotional patterns. Emotion, according to Dr Stone, *'is a blend of mind and senses. It is the etheric realm (the conscious mind operating through the senses) which seeks fulfilment of individual desires. Unfulfilled desires lead to pain, sorrow, effort and frustration.'* As we gain greater awareness of what lies behind our desires, our passion is turned into *com*passion.

Emotion can also be defined in terms of a conditioned response to a stimulus. The stimulus might be something someone says or does to us, or any set of circumstances. Examples of some circumstances which might bring up unpleasant emotions are: being rejected or unappreciated, losing your lob, ending a relationship being stuck in a traffic jam, etc. The list is endless. We all have conditioned responses to particular situations. This means we learned the response at an earlier time of life (usually childhood). This initial experience creates the emotion or thoughts and all it takes is a similar circumstance to bring the old feelings or actions. In counselling clients it is important to help them realise that they are responsible for their reactions (thoughts, emotions) and, consequently, they are the ultimate dictators of how they will feel.

Most of us have been raised in a way which fostered a negative self-image. All of the *'don't do this or that'* type of statement along with other parental criticisms, resulted in our thinking we were not acceptable. Not surprisingly, then, negative thoughts manifested themselves later in life. For example, our fear of rejection attracts people to us who are rejecting types. In order to overcome such fears we must see that we 'bought into' a belief system. In this sense our thoughts have no objective reality but rather a subjective reality in the way in which we have chosen to believe will indeed effect circumstances in our lives. Although this is merely an intellectual understanding of our predicament, such a consideration starts a process of mental and emotional unfolding which brings us into greater bodily realisation.

As we gain a better understanding of ourselves, the way in which we communicate with others takes on a deeper meaning. Learning to bring effective communication into our own lives is a profound method of growth. Effective communication results in problem resolution, greater self-confidence, a closer relationship with whomever you communicate with. It's not possible to learn effective communication merely by reading a book. It's an experience, a soul quality. True communication is an expression of love and acceptance and brings people closer together. Here are some guidelines that I have found useful. They are a result of my own experiences in life, as well as communication courses I have participated in and courses I have led and developed.

Firstly, remember that when we feel negative toward someone, it is because they present to us those aspects within ourselves with which we are not fully reconciled. They have been created by our thoughts to present us with what we need to work on, i.e., they have 'pushed our buttons' and evoked a conditioned response. When this negative response occurs, communicate to the person concerned how you feel, without blaming them for your feeling.

Example: "*I get angry when you come home late,*" as opposed to "*You make me angry when you come home late.*" When we blame someone he or she usually becomes defensive and an argument or hurt feelings occur. A response to a "*you make me*" statement might be:

"*Don't talk to me about being late. Remember the time you were ten minutes late? Did I object?... etc.*"

175

Here's an example of a communication which would most likely elicit an open, accepting response:

"You know, I'm not sure why, but I really get angry when you come home late. I guess as a child I was taught the importance of being punctual and I expect others to behave the same way. Also, I think I'm being a bit selfish in that I really wish I could spend more time with you. In any case, if you could call me if you know you are going to be late, that would be great. I do worry about you."

Can you see how this would make for more productive communication? I have found that when we avoid blaming others and, rather, put our own convictions under consideration, we leave them feeling as though they have a choice in their behaviour. And most people, by virtue of knowing that, however they behave, they are 'acceptable', will usually choose to do what brings people closer together. If I know someone will love (accept) me no matter what I do, I usually do what makes them and me happy.

Here are some other guidelines for effective communication:

TELL THE TRUTH
Lying doesn't work. It shows that you are still coming from a place of fear and attachment. It also hinders free communication in that you must always worry they will find out what you lied about. Truthful communication (not brutal honesty), done with love, always gets beneficial results.

TO CREATE A SAFE SPACE BE WILLING TO BE UNSAFE
Take chances, be truthful, express yourself without blame, despite the other person's reactions. In time they will take risks too. Try it and see.

KNOW YOUR INTENDED RESULT
This is the key to effective communication. If your intention is to resolve problems, become closer to the other person and create a greater acceptance of circumstances in your life, that is what will occur. Remember the law: your thoughts (intentions) create the result of those thoughts. If your intention is to blame, get even, hurt someone, then only bad feelings will occur. Closely examine what your intention is before you communicate.

DON'T TAKE THINGS PERSONALLY

As stated before, when someone is negative towards you it is their own conditioned response and something they must deal with. You just happened to push the right buttons. Each situation in life is an opportunity to grow and learn. Make the best of the situation. Give them the space they need in order to learn what they must learn.

In summation remember these three key points:

Love is accepting people as they are.
Happiness is related to your ability to accept things as they are.
True communication is an expression of love.

With a free flow of energy in our body we are able to feel the joy of simply being alive. But we cut off this flow when we become attached to our emotions and desires. We must learn that, as long as we hold external circumstances responsible for our happiness, we will never be free. As we learn to surrender that which blocks our energy (and remember it is completely our choice to do so) we arrive at a truer, deeper place within us and our fulfilment becomes an internal process independent of the impermanent, external world.

9 LOVE – THE SOURCE OF ALL ENERGY

Pierre Pannetier said that, *"Love is the essence of life everywhere in the Universe. To use this energy in health-building, we need to tune ourselves into it. It is the primary factor in Polarity Therapy."*

When speaking of this energy, the most powerful in the universe, we're referring to a love that is broader and more encompassing than the love between two people. It is unconditional, given without expecting anything in return, and it can be defined as the total acceptance (and forgiveness) of ourselves and others. It is said that God is love, and cultivating this love will make us healthier and happier.

Some practical ways I've found to express this form of love for my own health enhancement are as follows:

1 Avoid negative thoughts, words and actions - particularly such words as hate. These sentiments will only serve to perpetuate that negative experience. Like attracts like, so loving thoughts and actions will attract love.

2 When communicating some 'correction' (rather than criticism) to someone, do it with understanding and acceptance. If your correction alienates you from the person, it probably was not done with love. Ask yourself if your intention behind your words is to bring you closer to someone. It's important to be able to separate people from their flaws and actions; to be able to love someone while not necessarily appreciating his or her 'wrong-doing'.

3 Find the good and praise it. From the time we were children, most of us have experienced a great deal of criticism and blame. The result is that we've learned to be angry, defensive, unhappy and often lacking in self-esteem. We all need to be acknowledged and appreciated. If I find myself mentally judging or criticising someone, I look for something positive about that person - a quality, physical attribute, clothing, etc. - and praise it either mentally or verbally.

4 Learn to accept correction with a right attitude. Despite how it is given, benefit from it. St Francis of Assisi said, *"Learn to accept blame, criticism, and accusations silently without retaliation, even if it is untrue or unjustified."* If we can do this, our health and happiness will improve tenfold - so will the quality of our relationships.

5 If people come to you feeling depressed, find a way to uplift their spirits so they leave feeling happier about themselves and life.

6 Strive to change yourself.

7 Influence others by your own understanding, kindness and compassion.

8 Find satisfaction and joy in giving.

9 Learn to meditate. Meditation leads to peace which opens the heart to the inflow and outflow of Love.

In the words of Mahatma Gandhi, *"the only devils that exist are the ones running around in our own hearts."* When we work on freeing ourselves from these demons, such as negativity and fear, we allow the healing energy to flow freely, powered by the source of all energy - Love.

POSTSCRIPT - SPIRITUAL HEALING

Jesus said: "*Man shall not live by bread alone, but by every Word that proceedeth out of the mouth of God.*" The 'Word' refers to life energy or cosmic vibratory force. The 'mouth of God' is the medulla oblongata in the posterior part of the brain tapering off into the spinal cord. This is the area in the human body that life energy enters. It is this energy which creates, sustains, and heals us.

All external methods of healing such as medicine, massage, spinal adjustment, etc. only cooperate with the life energy and without it are unable to heal. Disease is really caused by the inaction of the life energy within us. When the cells or tissues which carry the energy are seriously damaged life energy withdraws from that area and illness begins.

External methods of healing such as food and medicine can chemically help the blood and cells. Their use is limited because they are external. The best methods are those that help the life energy to return and resume its internal healing processes. External methods are effective only if they can stimulate the life energy back to the diseased body part.

Healing with spirit is the superior method of healing. God or Spirit created life energy. This cosmic vibratory force is the same energy out of which we and everything else in the universe was created. It surrounds and permeates all of creation all the time. We can direct this cosmic energy into the medulla oblongata by using our will power. Energy, directed into the medulla gets distributed to the 5 chakras or spinal plexuses. Life energy in these whirling energy centres carry on the work of the sensory and motor nerves. It also charges the circulation, vitalises each blood cell, and feeds every nerve, which in turn, recharges the other cells of the body.

All of our cells are condensed energy and can be instantly renewed through strong will. The power of will bridges the gap between life energy in the body and the cosmic energy surrounding it. The greater your will power, the greater the flow of life energy into the body.

To successfully heal ourselves or others will power is the vital factor. As a healer your will to heal your patient should be very strong. When his or her receptivity to healing is as strong, then you are in harmony. You need their responsiveness in order to heal spiritually. For spiritual healing to occur, we have to develop our own consciousness so that we feel we live by Spirit. Most people live by 'bread' or food and identify their consciousness with heir bodies instead of with Spirit. The realisation that God manifests in us and in all of His creation as vibration or energy is a necessary step in healing. The only thing differentiating the various components of this material universe are vibratory rates. Ether, air, water, fire, earth, man, animals, consciousness, are all different rates of vibration.

Consciousness is intelligent vibration. This intelligence guides the aforementioned components to function according to a Divine order. It is evident everywhere in the universe.

Man is like a battery that is recharged by an electrical force or life energy. This life energy again, is what cures disease. An automobile battery needs chemicals and an electrical charge to function efficiently (e.g. be alive). Man also needs chemicals (food, water, oxygen and sunshine) and the charge of life energy to live. A dying battery cannot be revived by adding water and chemicals to it. It needs to be electrically recharged. Electricity acting on the chemicals constitute the life of a battery.

The cosmic electrical force in man is what keeps us alive. This force converts food, oxygen, and sunshine into living energy. Its intelligence enables it to convert food materials into different forms of tissue (adipose, cardiac, nerves, bones, muscle, etc.). This electricity or energy is finer in nature than solids and liquids and offer a more subtle force for healing. These finer forces affect the electronic constituency of the body and harmonise wrong vibratory conditions which gross medicines cannot reach. Rays of life energy can penetrate into the germ disturbed atomic composition of affected cells where medicines cannot.

The body is sustained by will power and energy. Will power brings energy from the outer cosmic source into the 'body battery' or the medulla oblongata. Our will can direct that energy to heal any body part. Here, then, is a simple technique and when practiced daily will prove its efficacy.

Tension of any muscle or body part is a result of energy being sent there by will power. *The greater the tension the greater the energy.*

First try this experiment:

1 Extend your right arm out in front of you.
2 Place your left hand on your right bicep.
3 Flex your right arm by bending it at the elbow. Feel the automatic contraction of the bicep muscle by movement of the arm.

Now try this:

1 Relax your right arm and let it hang at your side.
2 With your left hand, grasp the bicep muscle of the right arm.
3 Close your eyes.
4 Without bending your right arm at the elbow contract the bicep slowly to its maximum, using your will.
5 Relax.

In the first example, movement of the arm contracted the bicep muscle. In the second example, contraction was done by will power.

Points to remember in using this technique:

1 Close your eyes.
2 Concentrate deeply at the spiritual eye between your eyebrows. This is the centre of the will in man. By polarity it is opposite the medulla oblongata.
3 Contract the part of the body that needs healing.
4 Visualise life energy flowing into the body through the medulla and direct it to that body part.

For a more complete description of this technique see Self-healing visualisation p. 162

Additional Spiritual Exercises

Remember that all methods of healing are limited in their effectiveness unless one knows that their potency comes from the sole unlimited power of Spirit or God which is working behind them. His power of healing is almighty and sufficient in itself. When one is completely willing and enthusiastic with these spiritual exercises - without fail, healing can be instantaneous.

Mental Healing Exercise

May be done seated or lying down

1 Close your eyes.
2 Concentrate on both feet and visualise and feel warm electrical energy tingling over the soles of your feet.
3 Repeat this visualisation on the calves, thighs, hips, abdomen, intestines, navel,stomach, liver, kidneys, palms, forearms, upper arms, spine, chest, heart, throat, eyes, ears, nostrils, mouth, back of the head and top of the head.
4 Feel the tingling energy in every part.
5 Now concentrate your mind on the weak or diseased part.
6 Mentally chant OM and feel a warm electrical force being generated by the mental chanting of OM.
7 Chant OM 15 times as you concentrate on each weak or diseased body part.

Vital Healing Exercise

1 Close your eyes.
2 Inhale.
3 Hold your breath in your lungs and visualise it as a healing light.
4 Visualise it moving to the medulla oblongata and mixing with the cosmic life force entering your body.
5 Now concentrate the healing light at the point between the eyebrows.
6 Direct this energy to the diseased body part and feel it electrocuting the disease.
7 Exhale.

APPENDIX

**Charts from the writings of
Dr Randolph Stone the founder of Polarity Therapy**

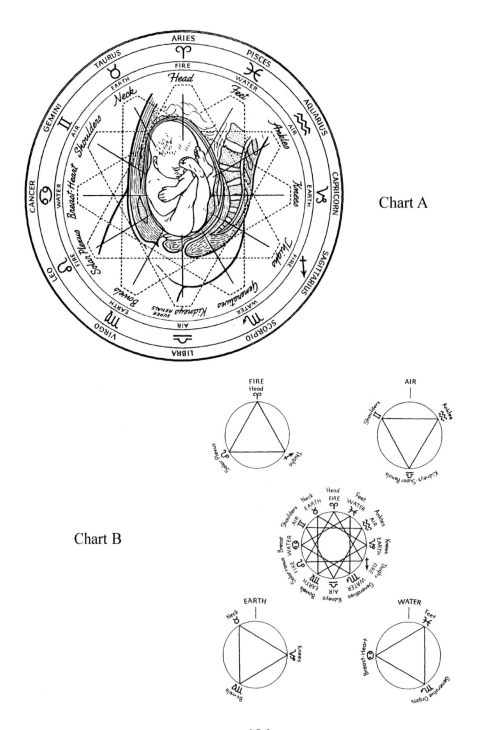

Chart A

Chart B

186

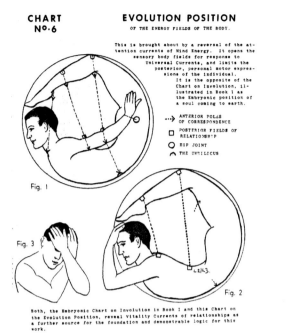

EVOLUTION POSITION
OF THE ENERGY FIELDS OF THE BODY.

This is brought about by a reversal of the attention currents of Mind Energy. It opens the
sensory body fields for response to
Universal Currents, and limits the
posterior, personal motor expres-
sions of the individual.
It is the opposite of the
Chart on Involution, il-
lustrated in Book I as
the Embryonic position of
a soul coming to earth.

- - -> ANTERIOR POLES
OF CORRESPONDENCE

□ POSTERIOR FIELDS OF
RELATIONSHIP

○ HIP JOINT

⌒ THE UMBILICUS

Chart C

Fig. 1

Fig. 3

Fig. 2

Both, the Embryonic Chart on Involution in Book I and this Chart on
the Evolution Position, reveal Vitality Currents of relationships as
a further source for the foundation and demonstrable logic for this
work.

Chart D

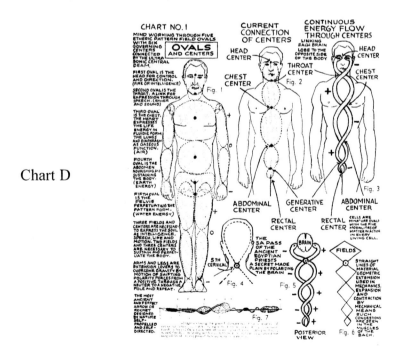

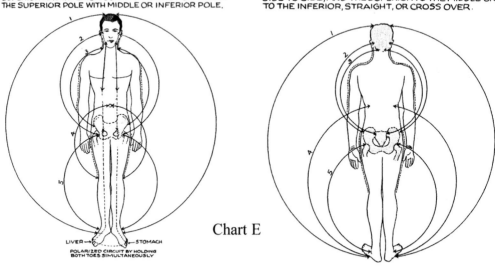

CHART NO.4.   GEOMETRIC ANTERIOR AND
LATERAL POLARITY REFLEXES AS POTENT
SUPERIOR AND INFERIOR CONTACT POINTS POLARIZING
THE SUPERIOR POLE WITH MIDDLE OR INFERIOR POLE.

LIVER ——— STOMACH
POLARIZED CIRCUIT BY HOLDING
BOTH TOES SIMULTANEOUSLY

Chart E

CHART NO.5.   POSTERIOR LATERAL GEOMETRICAL
POLARITY REFLEXES AND CONTACT POINTS FROM
SIDE TO SIDE, AND THE SUPERIOR TO THE MIDDLE OR
TO THE INFERIOR, STRAIGHT, OR CROSS OVER.

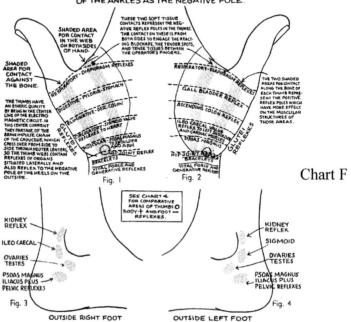

CHART NO.17.   THUMBS AS NEUTER REFLEXES EMBRACING THE ENTIRE
AREAS BELOW THE DIAPHRAGM ON EACH SIDE OF THE
BODY, COMPARED TO REFLEXES AROUND THE OUTSIDE
OF THE ANKLES AS THE NEGATIVE POLE.

Chart F

188

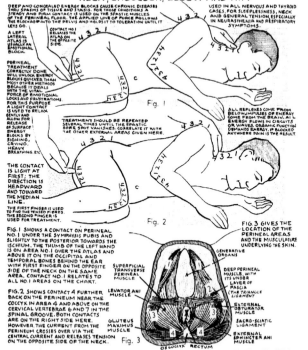

CHART NO.30. PERINEAL CONTACTS IN RELATION TO THE NECK, SHOULDER, ELBOW AND HIP.

DEEP AND CONCEALED ENERGY BLOCKS CAUSE CHRONIC DISEASES THRU SPASMS OF TISSUE AND STASIS. FOR THOSE CONDITIONS A STEADY AND FIRM CONTACT IS USED ON THE SPASTIC MUSCLES OF THE PERINEAL FLOOR. THE APPLIED LINE OF FORCE FOLLOWS THE BLOCKADE INTO THE PELVIS AND HOLDS IT TO TOLERATION UNTIL IT LETS GO.

A LEFT LATERAL ATLAS IS USUALLY AN EMOTIONAL BLOCK.

CONTACT NO.1 RELEASES THE ATLAS ON THE OPPOSITE SIDE.

PERINEAL TREATMENT CORRECTLY DONE WILL UNLOCK ENERGY BLOCKS QUICKER THAN MOST OTHER METHODS BECAUSE IT DEALS WITH THE VITAL FORCE OF EMOTIONAL LOCKS AND FRUSTRATIONS. FOR THIS PURPOSE A LIGHT CONTACT IS USED TO RELAX GENTLY AND ALLOW FOR RELEASE OF SURFACE ENERGY BLOCKS BY SIGHING, CRYING, HEAVY BREATHING, ETC.

THE CONTACT IS LIGHT AT FIRST; THE DIRECTION IS HEADWARD AND TOWARD THE MEDIAN LINE.

THE FIRST FINGER IS USED TO FIND THE TENSED FIBRES. THE SECOND FINGER IS USED FOR TREATMENT.

USED IN ALL NERVOUS AND THYROID CASES. FOR SLEEPLESSNESS, NECK AND GENERAL TENSION, ESPECIALLY IN NEURASTHENIA AND RESPIRATORY SYMPTOMS.

ALL REFLEXES COME FROM BELOW. IMPULSES OF ENERGY COME FROM THE BRAIN. ALL ENERGY FLOWS IN CIRCUITS OR WAVES. ORGANIC FUNCTION OBTAINS ENERGY. IF BLOCKED ANYWHERE PAIN IS THE RESULT.

Fig. 1

TREATMENT SHOULD BE REPEATED SEVERAL TIMES UNTIL THE SPASTIC SORE SPOT VANISHES. CORRELATE IT WITH THE OTHER EXTERNAL AREAS GIVEN HERE.

Fig. 2

FIG.1 SHOWS A CONTACT ON PERINEAL NO.1 UNDER THE SYMPHYSIS PUBIS AND SLIGHTLY TO THE POSTERIOR TOWARDS THE ISCHIUM. THE THUMB OF THE LEFT HAND IS ON AREA NO.1 OVER THE ATLAS AND ABOVE IT ON THE OCCIPITAL AND TEMPORAL BONES BEHIND THE EAR WITH FIRST FINGER ON THE OPPOSITE SIDE OF THE NECK ON THE SAME AREA. CONTACT NO.1 RELATES TO ALL NO.1 AREAS ON THE CHART.

FIG.2 SHOWS CONTACT 4 FURTHER BACK ON THE PERINEUM NEAR THE COCCYX IN AREA 4 AND ABOVE ON THE CERVICAL VERTEBRAE 6 AND 7 IN THE SPINAL GROOVE. BOTH CONTACTS ARE ON THE RIGHT SIDE HERE. HOWEVER THE CURRENT FROM THE PERINEUM CROSSES OVER VIA THE CENTRAL CURRENT AND RELEASES TENSION ON THE OPPOSITE SIDE OF THE NECK.

FIG.3 GIVES THE LOCATION OF THE PERINEAL AREAS AND THE MUSCULATURE UNDERLYING THE SKIN.

GENERATIVE ORGANS

SUPERFICIAL TRANSVERSE PERINEAL MUSCLE

DEEP PERINEAL MUSCLE WITH ITS UNDER LAYER OF FASCIA (THE TRIANGLE LIGAMENT)

LEVATOR ANI MUSCLE

EXTERNAL OBTURATOR MUSCLE

GLUTEUS MAXIMUS MUSCLE

SACRO-SCIATIC LIGAMENT

EXTERNAL SPHINCTER ANI MUSCLE

OS COCCYX   RECTUM

Fig. 3

Chart G

CHART FOR PERINEAL TREATMENT DESCRIBED ON PAGES 50, 51, 52 IN THE NEW ENERGY CONCEPT OF THE HEALING ART. PAGE 49 GIVES A DIAGRAM OF PERINEAL FLOOR AND CONTACT POINTS.

Chart H

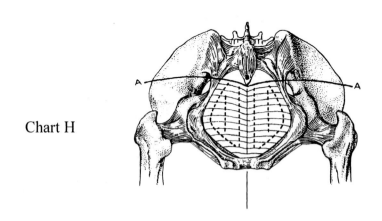

BIBLIOGRAPHY

Airola, Pavvo, N.D., *How to Get Well,* Health Plus Publishers, 1984.
Dr Airola's handbook of natural healing. It contains therapeutic uses of foods, vitamins, food supplements, juices, herbs, fasting, baths and other ancient and modern nutritional and biological modalities in the treatment of common ailments.

Bieler, Henry G, Food is Your Best Medicine, Ballantine Books.
A classic book on using natural foods to help heal a variety of illnesses.

Gandhi, Mahatma, Health Guide, Crossing Press, USA, 2000.
A most inspiring book which gives many helpful ideas on living a balanced life physically, mentally and spiritually. Subjects range from diet, exercise and sexuality to Gandhi's views on medicine and health.

Jensen, Bernard, Nature Has a Remedy, Keats Pub Inc, 2000.
The essence of fifty plus years of experience in natural healing with thousands of patients and students. These books are filled with Dr Jensen's inspiration and wisdom for enhancing health naturally.

Stone, Randolph, Polarity Therapy, **The Complete Collected Works Volume 1 & II**
CRCS Publications, Reno, U.S.A. The a 2-volume set by the originator of the system. All of Dr Stone's works contain a wealth of material on the subject of Polarity Therapy. They are very technical and are meant to be studied in depth. They are not easy to understand without a sufficient background in Polarity Therapy. Any serious student of Polarity Therapy would find them invaluable.

Yogananda, Paramahansa, Scientific Healing Affirmations, Self Realization Fellowship Publishers, Los Angeles, USA, 1986.
This wonderful little book covers the scientific use of concentration and affirmations for healing inharmonies of body, mind and soul through reason, will, feeling and prayer. Paramahansa Yogananda's teachings on health and healing are totally in harmony with Dr Stone's work in Polarity Therapy. I highly recommend anything written by Yogananda on the subject of health, diet, exercise, life energy, etc.

Other Books on Polarity Therapy

Dr Stone, Randolph, Health Building: CRCS Publications USA**.** A guide to exercise, nutrition and attitude by the founder of Polarity Therapy

Gordon, Richard, Your Healing Hands: The Polarity Experience, North Atlantic Press. USA. A good beginners guide to Polarity Therapy.

Young, Phil, The Art of Polarity Therapy: Prism Press, England and Masterworks International. A practitioners perspective on Polarity Therapy and in-depth look at the Structural aspects of the art.

Sills, Franklin, The Polarity Process: North Atlantic Press. USA. A more in depth introduction to the theory behind Polarity Therapy.

Burger, Bruce, Energy Anatomy: North Atlantic Press. USA. Detailed background and theory to Polarity Therapy including yogic perspective and sacred geometry.

Chitty, John, & Muller, Mary Louise, Energy Exercises: Polarity Press, Boulder USA Covers polarity theory and exercise.

Campbell, Morag, Quinta Essentia - The Five Elements: Masterworks International, England. Insights into the how the five elements manifest in body, mind and communication.

Seidman, Maruti, A Guide to Polarity Therapy - Gentle Art of Hands-on Healing North Atlantic Press. USA. A good introductory guide.

TREATMENT INDEX

For Training and Seminars on Polarity Therapy Worldwide

Contact Details

Masterworks International
Plunkett Chambers
21/23 Oliver Plunkett Street
Cork
Co.Cork
Ireland

Tel: 00353 (0) 86 3252645

Also available books, instructional DVD's and posters on Polarity Therapy. See web site for full details.

www. masterworksinternational.com

email: info@masterworksinternational.com